Kaplan Publishing are constantly finding new v
looking for exam success and our online reso
extra dimension to your studies.

CW00432131

This book comes with free MyKaplan online re
study anytime, anywhere. **This free online resource is not sold
separately and is included in the price of the book.**

Having purchased this book, you have access to the following online study materials:

CONTENT	AAT	
	Text	Kit
Electronic version of the book	✓	✓
Knowledge Check tests with instant answers	✓	
Mock assessments online	✓	✓
Material updates	✓	✓

How to access your online resources

Received this book as part of your Kaplan course?
If you have a MyKaplan account, your full online resources will be added automatically, in line with the information in your course confirmation email. If you've not used MyKaplan before, you'll be sent an activation email once your resources are ready.

Bought your book from Kaplan?
We'll automatically add your online resources to your MyKaplan account. If you've not used MyKaplan before, you'll be sent an activation email.

Bought your book from elsewhere?
Go to **www.mykaplan.co.uk/add-online-resources**
Enter the ISBN number found on the title page and back cover of this book.
Add the unique pass key number contained in the scratch panel below.
You may be required to enter additional information during this process to set up or confirm your account details.

This code can only be used once for the registration of this book online. This registration and your online content will expire when the examinations covered by this book have taken place. Please allow one hour from the time you submit your book details for us to process your request.

Please scratch the film to access your unique code.

Please be aware that this code is case-sensitive and you will need to include the dashes within the passcode, but not when entering the ISBN.

PUBLISHING

AAT

Q2022

Drafting and Interpreting Financial Statements

EXAM KIT

This Exam Kit supports study for the following AAT qualifications:
AAT Level 4 Diploma in Professional Accounting
AAT Diploma in Professional Accounting at SCQF Level 8

PUBLISHING

British Library Cataloguing-in-Publication Data

A catalogue record for this book is available from the British Library.

Published by:

Kaplan Publishing UK

Unit 2 The Business Centre

Molly Millar's Lane

Wokingham

Berkshire

RG41 2QZ

ISBN: 978-1-83996-589-0

© Kaplan Financial Limited, 2023

Printed and bound in Great Britain.

CONTENTS

	Page

This document references IFRS® Standards and IAS® Standards, which are authored by the International Accounting Standards Board (the Board), and published in the 2020 IFRS Standards Blue Book.

Features in this exam kit

In addition to providing a wide ranging bank of real exam style questions, we have also included in this kit:

- unit-specific information and advice on exam technique

- our recommended approach to make your revision for this particular unit as effective as possible.

You will find a wealth of other resources to help you with your studies on the AAT website:

www.aat.org.uk/

Quality and accuracy are of the utmost importance to us so if you spot an error in any of our products, please send an email to mykaplanreporting@kaplan.com with full details, or follow the link to the feedback form in MyKaplan.

Our Quality Co-ordinator will work with our technical team to verify the error and take action to ensure it is corrected in future editions.

UNIT-SPECIFIC INFORMATION

THE EXAM

FORMAT OF THE ASSESSMENT

The assessment will comprise of seven independent tasks. Students will be assessed by computer-based assessment.

In any one assessment, students may not be assessed on all content, or on the full depth or breadth of a piece of content. The content assessed may change over time to ensure validity of assessment, but all assessment criteria will be tested over time.

The learning outcomes for this unit are as follows:

	Learning outcome	Weighting
1	Understand the reporting frameworks that underpin financial reporting	7%
2	Draft statutory financial statements for a limited company	43%
3	Draft consolidated financial statements	25%
4	Interpret financial statements using ratio analysis	25%
	Total	**100%**

Time allowed

2.5 hours

PASS MARK

The pass mark for all AAT CBAs is 70%.

 Always keep your eye on the clock and make sure you attempt all questions!

DETAILED SYLLABUS

The detailed syllabus and study guide written by the AAT can be found at:

www.aat.org.uk/

INDEX TO QUESTIONS AND ANSWERS

EXAM TECHNIQUE

- **Do not skip any of the material** in the syllabus.

- **Read each question** *very* carefully.

- **Double-check your answer** before committing yourself to it.

- Answer **every** question – if you do not know an answer to a multiple choice question or true/false question, you don't lose anything by guessing. Think carefully before you **guess**.

- If you are answering a multiple-choice question, **eliminate first those answers that you know are wrong**. Then choose the most appropriate answer from those that are left.

- **Don't panic** if you realise you've answered a question incorrectly. Getting one question wrong will not mean the difference between passing and failing.

Computer-based exams – tips

- Do not attempt a CBA until you have **completed all study material** relating to it.

- On the AAT website there is a CBA demonstration. It is **ESSENTIAL** that you attempt this before your real CBA. You will become familiar with how to move around the CBA screens and the way that questions are formatted, increasing your confidence and speed in the actual exam.

- Be sure you understand how to use the **software** before you start the exam. If in doubt, ask the assessment centre staff to explain it to you.

- Questions are **displayed on the screen** and answers are entered using keyboard and mouse. At the end of the exam, you are given a certificate showing the result you have achieved.

- In addition to the traditional multiple-choice question type, CBAs will also contain **other types of questions**, such as number entry questions, drag and drop, true/false, pick lists or drop down menus or hybrids of these.

- In some CBAs you will have to type in complete computations or written answers.

- You need to be sure you **know how to answer questions** of this type before you sit the exam, through practise.

KAPLAN'S RECOMMENDED REVISION APPROACH

QUESTION PRACTICE IS THE KEY TO SUCCESS

Success in professional examinations relies upon you acquiring a firm grasp of the required knowledge at the tuition phase. In order to be able to do the questions, knowledge is essential.

However, the difference between success and failure often hinges on your exam technique on the day and making the most of the revision phase of your studies.

The **Kaplan Study Text** is the starting point, designed to provide the underpinning knowledge to tackle all questions. However, in the revision phase, poring over text books is not the answer.

Kaplan Pocket Notes are designed to help you quickly revise a topic area; however you then need to practise questions. There is a need to progress to exam style questions as soon as possible, and to tie your exam technique and technical knowledge together.

The importance of question practice cannot be over-emphasised.

The recommended approach below is designed by expert tutors in the field, in conjunction with their knowledge of the examiner and the specimen assessment.

You need to practise as many questions as possible in the time you have left.

OUR AIM

Our aim is to get you to the stage where you can attempt exam questions confidently, to time, in a closed book environment, with no supplementary help (i.e. to simulate the real examination experience).

Practising your exam technique is also vitally important for you to assess your progress and identify areas of weakness that may need more attention in the final run up to the examination.

In order to achieve this we recognise that initially you may feel the need to practice some questions with open book help.

Good exam technique is vital.

THE KAPLAN REVISION PLAN

Stage 1: Assess areas of strengths and weaknesses

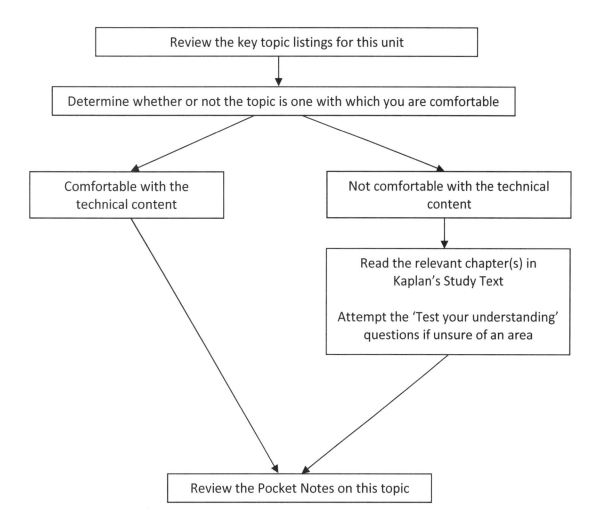

Stage 2: Practice questions

Follow the order of revision of topics as presented in this Kit and attempt the questions in the order suggested.

Try to avoid referring to Study Texts and your notes and the model answer until you have completed your attempt.

Review your attempt with the model answer and assess how much of the answer you achieved.

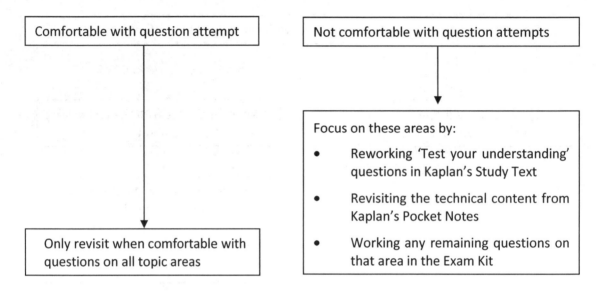

Stage 3: Final pre-exam revision

We recommend that you **attempt at least one mock examination** containing a set of previously unseen exam-standard questions.

Attempt the mock CBA online in timed, closed book conditions to simulate the real exam experience.

Section 1

PRACTICE QUESTIONS

STATUTORY FINANCIAL STATEMENTS FOR A LIMITED COMPANY

1   ABC LTD

DATA

You have been asked to help prepare the financial statements of ABC Ltd for the year ended 31 October 20X9. The company's trial balance as at 31 October 20X9 is shown below.

ABC Ltd

Trial balance as at 31 October 20X9

	Debit	Credit
	£000	£000
8% bank loan repayable 20Y6		28,000
Accruals		292
Administrative expenses	6,888	
Cash at bank	19,308	
Distribution costs	4,900	
Final dividend for year ended 31 October 20X9	1,080	
Interest	1,120	
Interim dividend for year ended 31 October 20X9	780	
Inventories as at 1 November 20X8	8,932	
Property, plant and equipment – cost	79,760	
Accumulated depreciation at 31 October 20X9		43,560
Purchases	65,552	
Retained earnings		6,930
Returns inwards	688	
Returns outwards		446
Sales		93,554
Share capital		18,000
Trade and other payables		2,694
Trade and other receivables	4,468	
	————	————
	193,476	193,476
	————	————

Additional data

- The share capital of the company consists of ordinary shares with a nominal value of £1.

- The inventories at the close of business on 31 October 20X9 were valued at £9,974,000.

- The company paid £1,024,000 for one year's insurance on 1 February 20X9; this is due to expire on 31 January 20Y0 (i.e. next year).

- The company hired vehicles to distribute finished goods locally. It was able to negotiate a deal with a local company for the period 1 September to 30 November 20X9 at a cost of £198,000. This was invoiced on 6 November 20X9 and paid, in full, on 1 December 20X9. No entry has been made in the accounts.

- Interest on the bank loan for the last six months of the year has not been included in the accounts in the trial balance.

- The company made a bonus issue of 2,500,000 ordinary shares out of retained earnings but has not made any accounting entries for this.

- The tax charge for the year has been calculated as £1,960,000.

(a) **Draft the statement of profit or loss and other comprehensive income for ABC Ltd for the year ended 31 October 20X9.**

(b) **Draft the statement of financial position for ABC Ltd as at the 31 October 20X9.**

(c) **Draft the statement of changes in equity for ABC Ltd for the year ended 31 October 20X9.**

Note: Additional notes and disclosures are not required.

Journal entries for the additional data:

	Dr	Cr
	£000	£000

(a) **Statement of profit or loss for the year ended 31/10/X9**

	£000
Continuing operations	
Revenue	
	————
Gross profit	
	————
Profit from operations	
	————
Profit before tax	
	————
Profit for the period from continuing operations	
Other comprehensive income for the year	
	————
Total comprehensive income for the year	
	————

Workings

(W1) Revenue

	£000
Total	

(W2) COS

	£000
Total	

(W3) Distribution costs

	£000
Total	

(W4) Administrative expenses

	£000
Total	

(W5) Finance costs

	£000
Total	

(b)   Statement of financial position as at 31/10/X9

	£000
ASSETS	
Non-current assets	
	————
Current assets	
	————
	————
Total assets	
	————

EQUITY AND LIABILITIES	
	————
Total equity	
	————
Non-current liabilities	
	————
	————
Current liabilities	
	————
	————
Total liabilities	
	————
Equity and liabilities	
	————

Workings

(W1) PPE

	£000
Total	

(W2) Trade and other receivables

	£000
Total	

(W3) Retained earnings

	£000
Total	

(W4) Trade and other payables

	£000
Total	

(c) Statement of changes in equity

	Share capital	Share premium	Revaluation surplus	Retained earnings	Total
Bal b/f					
Bal c/f					

2   WILLOW LTD

DATA

You have been asked to help prepare the financial statements of Willow Ltd for the year ended 30 June 20X1. The company's trial balance as at 30 June 20X1 is shown below.

WILLOW LTD

Trial balance as at 30 June 20X1

	Debit £000	Credit £000
Share capital		50,000
Share premium		25,000
Revaluation surplus at 1 July 20X0		10,000
Land and buildings – value/cost	120,000	
accumulated depreciation at 1 July 20X0		22,500
Plant and equipment – cost	32,000	
accumulated depreciation at 1 July 20X0		18,000
Trade and other receivables	20,280	
Trade and other payables		8,725
5% bank loan repayable 20X5		20,000
Cash and cash equivalents	2,213	
Retained earnings at 1 July 20X0		12,920
Sales		100,926
Purchases	67,231	
Distribution costs	8,326	
Administrative expenses	7,741	
Inventories at 1 July 20X0	7,280	
Dividends paid	3,000	
	268,071	268,071

Further information:

- The inventories at the close of business on 30 June 20X1 cost £9,420,000.

- Depreciation is to be provided for the year to 30 June 20X1 as follows:

   Buildings   4% per annum   Straight line basis

   This should all be charged to administrative expenses

   Plant and equipment   20% per annum   Reducing balance basis

   This is to be apportioned as follows:

	%
Cost of sales	70
Distribution costs	20
Administrative expenses	10

   Land, which is non-depreciable, is included in the trial balance at a value of £40,000,000 and it is to be revalued to £54,000,000. This revaluation is to be included in the financial statements for the year ended 30 June 20X1.

- It has been decided to write off a debt of £540,000, which will be charged to administrative expenses.

- Included within distribution costs is £2,120,000 relating to an advertising campaign that will run from 1 January 20X1 to 31 December 20X1.

- The loan interest has not yet been accounted for.

- The tax charge for the year has been calculated as £2,700,000.

(a) **Draft the statement of profit or loss and other comprehensive income for Willow Ltd for the year ended 30 June 20X1.**

(b) **Draft the statement of financial position for Willow Ltd as at 30 June 20X1.**

Note: Additional notes and disclosures are not required.

(a) **Willow Ltd – Statement of profit or loss and other comprehensive income for the year ended 30 June 20X1**

	£000
Continuing operations	
Revenue	
	————
Gross profit	
	————
Profit from operations	
	————
Profit before tax	
	————
Profit for the period from continuing operations	
Other comprehensive income for the year	
	————
Total comprehensive income for the year	
	————

Workings

(W1) COS

	£000
Total	

(W2) Distribution costs

	£000
Total	

(W3) Administrative expenses

	£000
Total	

(W4) Finance costs

	£000
Total	

(W5) Revaluation

	£000
Total	

(b) **Willow Ltd – Statement of financial position as at 30 June 20X1**

	£000
ASSETS	
Non-current assets	
	————
Current assets	
	————
	————
Total assets	
	————
EQUITY AND LIABILITIES	
	————
Total equity	
	————
Non-current liabilities	
	————
	————
Current liabilities	
	————
	————
Total liabilities	
	————
Equity and liabilities	
	————

Workings

(W1) PPE

	£000
Total	

(W2) Trade and other receivables

	£000
Total	

(W3) Retained earnings

	£000
Total	

(W4) Trade and other payables

	£000
Total	

3   CLERC LTD

DATA

You have been asked to help prepare the financial statements of Clerc Ltd for the year ended 31 December 20X9. The company's trial balance as at 31 December 20X9 is shown below.

CLERC LTD

Trial balance as at 31 December 20X9

	Debit £	Credit £
Share capital		100,000
Share premium		20,000
Revaluation surplus at 1 January 20X9		50,000
Trade and other payables		13,882
Land and buildings – value/cost	210,000	
accumulated depreciation at 1 January 20X9		30,000
Plant and equipment – cost	88,000	
accumulated depreciation at 1 January 20X9		16,010
Trade and other receivables	8,752	
Accruals		3,029
5% bank loan repayable 20Y3		40,000
Cash and cash equivalents	6,993	
Retained earnings at 1 January 20X9		23,893
Sales		178,833
Purchases	130,562	
Distribution costs	7,009	
Administrative expenses	7,100	
Inventories at 1 January 20X9	17,331	
Bank interest received		100
	475,747	475,747

Further information:

- The interest for the year on the bank loan has not yet been paid or accrued.

- Land, which is non-depreciable, is included in the trial balance at a value of £110,000. On the 31 December 20X9, it was revalued to £150,000 and this revaluation is to be included in the financial statements.

- Depreciation is to be provided for the year to 31 December 20X9 as follows:

Buildings	10% per annum	Straight line basis
Plant and equipment	20% per annum	Reducing balance basis

Depreciation on plant and equipment should be charged to cost of sales. As part of the building contains the office accommodation, the depreciation for the 'Buildings' is apportioned as follows:

	%
Cost of sales	40
Administrative expenses	60

- Included in trade receivables is a balance of £1,720 that is considered to be irrecoverable due to the customer going into administration and the Directors of Clerc Ltd feel this should be written off.

- The inventories at the close of business on 31 December 20X9 were valued at cost of £19,871.

- Included in this balance was an inventory line costing £4,000 that, due to change in legislation, is now illegal. Clerc Ltd could rectify the items at a cost of £2,500 and plans to do so. The items usually retail to customers at £6,000.

- The tax charge for the year has been calculated as £7,162.

(a) **Draft the statement of profit or loss and other comprehensive income for Clerc Ltd for the year ended 31 December 20X9.**

(b) **Draft the statement of financial position for Clerc Ltd as at 31 December 20X9.**

   Note: Additional notes and disclosures are not required.

(a) **Clerc Ltd – Statement of profit or loss and other comprehensive income for the year ended 31 December 20X9**

	£000
Continuing operations	
Revenue	
	————
	————
Profit from operations	
	————
Profit before tax	
	————
Profit for the period from continuing operations	
Other comprehensive income for the year	
	————
Total comprehensive income for the year	
	————

Workings

(W1) COS

	£000
Total	

(W2) Administrative expenses

	£000
Total	

(W3) Finance costs

	£000
Total	

(W4) Revaluation

	£000
Total	

(b) **Clerc Ltd – Statement of financial position as at 31 December 20X9**

	£000
ASSETS	
Non-current assets	
	———
Current assets	
	———
	———
Total assets	
	———
EQUITY AND LIABILITIES	
	———
Total equity	
	———
Non-current liabilities	
	———
	———
Current liabilities	
	———
	———
Total liabilities	
	———
Equity and liabilities	
	———

Workings

(W1) PPE

	£000
Total	

(W2) Trade and other receivables

	£000
Total	

(W3) Retained earnings

	£000
Total	

(W4) Trade and other payables

	£000
Total	

4 RCH LTD

DATA

You have been asked to help prepare the financial statements of RCH Ltd for the year ended 31 March 20X1. The company's trial balance as at 31 March 20X1 is shown below.

RCH LTD

Trial balance as at 31 March 20X1

	Debit	Credit
	£	£
Share capital		50,000
Revaluation surplus at 1 April 20X0		12,500
Trade and other payables		25,342
Land and buildings – value/cost	281,450	
accumulated depreciation at 1 April 20X0		65,332
Plant and equipment – cost	94,400	
accumulated depreciation at 1 April 20X0		14,500
Trade and other receivables	12,176	
Accruals		1,217
7% bank loan repayable 20X8		26,000
Cash and cash equivalents		848
Retained earnings		12,017
Interest paid	910	
Sales		480,742
Purchases	153,444	
Distribution costs	23,587	
Administrative expenses	36,811	
Inventories at 1 April 20X0	84,220	
Dividends paid	1,500	
	688,498	688,498

Further information:

- The inventories at the close of business on 31 March 20X1 cost £77,004.

- Depreciation is to be provided for the year to 31 March 20X1 as follows:

Buildings	4% per annum	Straight line basis
Plant and equipment	25% per annum	Reducing balance basis

Depreciation is apportioned as follows:

	%
Cost of sales	60
Distribution costs	15
Administrative expenses	25

Land, which is non-depreciable, is included in the trial balance at a value of £100,000. It has recently been revalued at £151,000. This revaluation is to be included in the financial statements for the year ended 31 March 20X1.

- Trade receivables include a debt of £840, which is to be written off. Irrecoverable debts are charged to administrative expenses.

- RCH Ltd has not yet accrued for the unpaid loan interest.

- Distribution costs of £4,567 owing at 31 March 20X1 are to be accrued.

- The tax charge for the year has been calculated as £33,740.

(a)   **Draft the statement of profit or loss and other comprehensive income for RCH Ltd for the year ended 31 March 20X1.**

(b)   **Draft the statement of financial position for RCH Ltd as at 31 March 20X1.**

   Note: Additional notes and disclosures are not required.

(a)   **RCH Ltd – Statement of profit or loss and other comprehensive income for the year ended 31 March 20X1**

	£
Continuing operations	
Revenue	
	————
Gross profit	
	————
Profit from operations	
	————
Profit before tax	
	————
Profit for the period from continuing operations	
Other comprehensive income for the year	
	————
Total comprehensive income for the year	
	————

Workings

(W1) COS

	£000
Total	

(W2) Distribution costs

	£000
Total	

(W3) Administrative expenses

	£000
Total	

(W4) Finance costs

	£000
Total	

(W5) Revaluation

	£000
Total	

(b) **RCH Ltd – Statement of financial position as at 31 March 20X1**

	£000
ASSETS	
Non-current assets	
	——————
Current assets	
	——————
	——————
Total assets	
	——————
EQUITY AND LIABILITIES	
	——————
Total equity	
	——————
Non-current liabilities	
	——————
	——————
Current liabilities	
	——————
	——————
Total liabilities	
	——————
Equity and liabilities	
	——————

Workings

(W1) PPE

	£000
Total	

(W2) Trade and other receivables

	£000
Total	

(W3) Retained earnings

	£000
Total	

(W4) Trade and other payables

	£000
Total	

5 MAGNOLIA LTD

DATA

You have been asked to prepare the statement of cash flows and statement of changes in equity for Magnolia Ltd for the year ended 31 March 20X1.

The most recent statement of profit or loss and other comprehensive income and statement of financial position (with comparatives for the previous year) of Magnolia Ltd are set out below.

Magnolia Ltd – Statement of profit or loss and other comprehensive income for the year ended 31 March 20X1.

	£000
Revenue	107,520
Cost of sales	(59,140)
Gross profit	48,380
Dividends received	280
Loss on disposal of property, plant and equipment	(575)
Distribution costs	(22,580)
Administrative expenses	(10,752)
Profit from operations	14,753
Finance costs	(1,052)
Profit before tax	13,701
Tax	(3,840)
Profit for the period	9,861

Magnolia Ltd – Statement of financial position as at 31 March 20X1

	20X1 £000	20X0 £000
ASSETS		
Non-current assets		
Property, plant and equipment	62,936	50,216
Current assets		
Inventories	14,194	11,827
Trade and other receivables	10,752	12,902
Cash and cash equivalents	672	0
	25,618	24,729
Total assets	88,554	74,945
EQUITY AND LIABILITIES		
Equity		
Share capital	10,800	7,200
Share premium	7,200	4,800
Retained earnings	57,200	48,539
Total equity	75,200	60,539
Non-current liabilities		
Bank loans	3,600	1,200
	3,600	1,200
Current liabilities		
Trade payables	5,914	10,644
Tax liabilities	3,840	2,130
Bank overdraft	0	432
	9,754	13,206
Total liabilities	13,354	14,406
Total equity and liabilities	88,554	74,945

Further information:

- The total depreciation charge for the year was £6,700,000.

- Property, plant and equipment costing £2,100,000 with accumulated depreciation of £800,000 were sold in the year.

- A dividend of £1,200,000 was paid during the year.

- Included in trade payables is £85,000 (20X0 £78,000) relating to interest payable.

(a) **Prepare a reconciliation of profit from operations to net cash from operating activities (starting with profit before tax) for Magnolia Ltd for the year ended 31 March 20X1.**

(b) **Prepare the statement of cash flows for Magnolia Ltd for the year ended 31 March 20X1.**

(c) **Draft the statement of changes in equity for Magnolia Ltd for the year ended 31 March 20X1.**

(a) **Reconciliation of profit from operations to net cash from operating activities**

	£000
Profit before tax	
Adjustments for:	
	———
Cash generated by operations	
	———
Net cash from operating activities	
	———

(b) Magnolia Ltd – Statement of cash flows for year ended 31 March 20X1

	£000
Net cash from operating activities	
Investing activities	
	———
Net cash used in investing activities	
Financing activities	
	———
Net cash from financing activities	
Net increase/(decrease) in cash and cash equivalents	
Cash and cash equivalents at beginning of year	
	———
Cash and cash equivalents at end of year	
	———

(c) Magnolia Ltd – Statement of changes in equity for the year ended 31 March 20X1

	Share capital	Other reserves	Retained earnings	Total equity
Balance at 1 April 20X0				
Changes in equity for 20X1				
	———	———	———	———
Balance at 31 March 20X1				
	———	———	———	———

Workings

(W1) Changes in working capital

	£000 20X0	£000 20X1	Increase/ Decrease

(W2) Interest paid

	£000
Total	

(W3) Proceeds on disposal of PPE

	£000
Total	

(W4) Tax paid

	£000
Total	

(W5) Purchase of PPE

	£000
Purchase of PPE	

(W6) Bank loans raised/redeemed

	£000 20X0	£000 20X1	Increase/ Decrease
Bank loans			

(W7) Share issue

	£000 20X0	£000 20X1	Increase/ Decrease
Share capital			
Share premium			
Total			

6 THORNGUMBALD LTD

DATA

You have been asked to prepare the statement of cash flows and statement of changes in equity for Thorngumbald Ltd for the year ended 31 March 20X9.

The most recent statement of profit or loss and other comprehensive income and statement of financial position (with comparatives for the previous year) of Thorngumbald Ltd are set out below.

Thorngumbald Ltd – Statement of profit or loss and other comprehensive income for the year ended 31 March 20X9

	£000
Revenue	89,600
Cost of sales	(49,280)
Gross profit	40,320
Dividends received	240
Gain on disposal of property, plant and equipment	896
Distribution costs	(18,816)
Administrative expenses	(8,960)
Profit from operations	13,680
Finance costs	(210)
Profit before tax	13,470
Tax	(5,768)
Profit for the period	7,702

Thorngumbald Ltd – Statement of financial position as at 31 March 20X9

	20X9	20X8
	£000	£000
ASSETS		
Non-current assets		
Property, plant and equipment	55,780	42,680
Current assets		
Inventories	11,828	9,856
Trade and other receivables	8,960	10,752
Cash and cash equivalents	560	0
	21,348	20,608
Total assets	**77,128**	**63,288**
EQUITY AND LIABILITIES		
Equity		
Share capital	9,000	6,000
Share premium	6,000	4,000
Retained earnings	48,432	41,284
Total equity	**63,432**	**51,284**
Non-current liabilities		
Bank loans	3,000	1,000
	3,000	1,000
Current liabilities		
Trade payables	4,928	8,870
Tax liabilities	5,768	1,774
Bank overdraft	0	360
	10,696	11,004
Total liabilities	**13,696**	**12,004**
Total equity and liabilities	**77,128**	**63,288**

Additional data

- The total depreciation charged for the year was £8,916,000.

- Property, plant and equipment costing £1,756,000 with accumulated depreciation of £668,000 were sold in the year.

- All sales and purchases were on credit. Other expenses were paid in cash.

- A dividend of £554,000 was paid during the year.

(a) **Prepare a reconciliation of profit from operations to net cash from operating activities (starting with profit before tax) for Thorngumbald Ltd for the year ended 31 March 20X9.**

(b) **Prepare the statement of cash flows for Thorngumbald Ltd for the year ended 31 March 20X9.**

(c) **Draft the statement of changes in equity for Thorngumbald Ltd for the year ended 31 March 20X9.**

(a) **Thorngumbald Ltd – Reconciliation of profit from operations to net cash from operating activities**

	£000
Profit before tax	
Adjustments for:	
	———
Cash generated by operations	
	———
Net cash from operating activities	
	———

(b)   Thorngumbald Ltd – Statement of cash flows for year ended 31 March 20X9

	£000
Net cash from operating activities	
Investing activities	
	————
Net cash used in investing activities	
Financing activities	
	————
Net cash from financing activities	
	————
Net increase/(decrease) in cash and cash equivalents	
Cash and cash equivalents at beginning of year	
	————
Cash and cash equivalents at end of year	
	————

(c)   Thorngumbald Ltd – Statement of changes in equity for the year ended 31 March 20X9

	Share capital	Other reserves	Retained earnings	Total equity
Balance at 1 April 20X8				
Changes in equity for 20X9				
	————	————	————	————
Balance at 31 March 20X9				
	————	————	————	————

Workings

(W1) Changes in working capital

	£000 20X8	£000 20X9	Increase/ Decrease

(W2) Proceeds on disposal of PPE

	£000

(W3) Purchase of PPE

	£000
Purchase of PPE	

(W4) Bank loans raised/redeemed

	£000 20X8	£000 20X9	Increase/ Decrease
Bank loans			

(W5) Share issue

	£000 20X8	£000 20X9	Increase/ Decrease
Share capital			
Share premium			
Total			

7   DEAN LTD

DATA

You have been asked to prepare the statement of cash flows and statement of changes in equity for Dean Ltd for the year ended 31 March 20X9.

The most recent statement of profit or loss and other comprehensive income and statement of financial position (with comparatives for the previous year) of Dean Ltd are set out below.

Dean Ltd – Statement of profit or loss and other comprehensive income for the year ended 31 March 20X9

	£000
Revenue	99,500
Cost of sales	(63,200)
	———
Gross profit	36,300
Gain on disposal of PPE	1,200
Distribution costs	(12,300)
Administrative expenses	(7,200)
	———
Profit from operations	18,000
Investment income	
– Dividends received	2,000
– Interest received	300
Finance costs	(1,200)
	———
Profit before tax	19,100
Tax	(3,820)
	———
Profit for the period	**15,280**
	———

Dean Ltd – Statement of financial position as at 31 March 20X9

	20X9	20X8
	£000	£000
ASSETS		
Non-current assets		
Property, plant and equipment	79,820	68,200
Current assets		
Inventories	10,300	12,100
Trade and other receivables	16,280	14,320
Cash and cash equivalents	0	935
	26,580	27,355
Total assets	106,400	95,555
EQUITY AND LIABILITIES		
Equity		
Share capital	30,000	25,000
Share premium	5,000	2,000
Revaluation surplus	5,000	0
Retained earnings	45,830	35,550
Total equity	85,830	62,550
Non-current liabilities		
Bank loans	5,000	15,000
	5,000	15,000
Current liabilities		
Trade payables	9,500	14,505
Tax liabilities	5,500	3,500
Bank overdraft	570	0
	15,570	18,005
Total liabilities	20,570	33,005
Total equity and liabilities	106,400	95,555

Further information:

- The total depreciation charge for the year was £6,235,000.

- Property, plant and equipment were sold during the year for £13,100,000. The items had originally cost £20,000,000 and had accumulated depreciation of £8,100,000 at the date of sale.

- All sales and purchases were on credit. Other expenses were paid for in cash.

- A dividend was paid out of retained earnings for the year.

(a) **Prepare a reconciliation of profit from operations to net cash from operating activities (starting with profit before tax) for Dean Ltd for the year ended 31 March 20X9.**

(b) **Prepare the statement of cash flows for Dean Ltd for the year ended 31 March 20X9.**

(c) **Draft the statement of changes in equity for Dean Ltd for the year ended 31 March 20X9.**

(a) **Reconciliation of profit from operations to net cash from operating activities**

	£000
Profit before tax	
Adjustments for:	
	———
Cash generated by operations	
	———
Net cash from operating activities	
	———

(b) Dean Ltd – Statement of cash flows for year ended 31 March 20X9

	£000
Net cash from operating activities	
Investing activities	
	———
Net cash used in investing activities	
Financing activities	
	———
Net cash from financing activities	
Net increase/(decrease) in cash and cash equivalents	
Cash and cash equivalents at beginning of year	
	———
Cash and cash equivalents at end of year	
	———

(c) Dean Ltd – Statement of changes in equity for the year ended 31 March 20X9

	Share capital	Share premium	Revaln reserve	Retained earnings	Total equity
Balance at 1 April 20X8					
Changes in equity for 20X9					
	———	———	———	———	———
Balance at 31 March 20X9					
	———	———	———	———	———

Workings

(W1) Changes in working capital

	£000 20X8	£000 20X9	Increase/ Decrease

(W2) Gain/loss on disposal of PPE

	£000

(W3) Purchase of PPE

	£000
Purchase of PPE	

(W4) Bank loans raised/redeemed

	£000 20X8	£000 20X9	Increase/ Decrease
Bank loans			

(W5) Share issue

	£000 20X8	£000 20X9	Increase/ Decrease
Share capital			
Share premium			
Total			

(W6) Dividends paid

	£000

8   **ROSSINGTON LTD**

DATA

You have been asked to prepare the statement of cash flows and statement of changes in equity for Rossington Ltd for the year ended 31 March 20X1.

The most recent statement of profit or loss and other comprehensive income and statement of financial position (with comparatives for the previous year) of Rossington Ltd are set out below.

Rossington Ltd – Statement of profit or loss and other comprehensive income for the year ended 31 March 20X1

Continuing operations	£000
Revenue	1,397
Cost of sales	(1,110)
	———
Gross profit	287
Dividends received	20
Distribution costs	(25)
Administrative expenses	(100)
	———
Profit from operations	182
Finance costs	(40)
	———
Profit before tax	142
Tax	(57)
	———
Profit for the period from continuing operations	85
	———

Rossington Ltd – Statement of financial position as at 31 March 20X1

	20X1	20X0
	£000	£000
ASSETS		
Non-current assets		
Property, plant and equipment	1,565	1,065
Current assets		
Inventories	480	510
Trade and other receivables	350	435
Cash	0	35
	830	980
Total assets	2,395	2,045
EQUITY AND LIABILITIES		
Equity		
£1 Share capital	500	300
£1 Share premium	150	85
Retained earnings	1,010	990
Total equity	1,660	1,375
Non-current liabilities		
Bank loans	300	25
	300	25
Current liabilities		
Trade payables	350	555
Tax liabilities	60	50
Bank overdraft	25	40
	435	645
Total liabilities	735	670
Total equity and liabilities	2,395	2,045

Further information:

- The total depreciation charge for the year was £255,000.

- During the year, plant with a carrying amount of £12,000 was sold for £15,000. The profit on disposal has been included within admin expenses.

- All sales and purchases were on credit. Other expenses were paid for in cash.

- A dividend was paid during the year.

(a) **Prepare a reconciliation of profit from operations to net cash from operating activities (starting with profit before tax) for Rossington Ltd for the year ended 31 March 20X1.**

(b) **Prepare the statement of cash flows for Rossington Ltd for the year ended 31 March 20X1.**

(c) **Draft the statement of changes in equity for Rossington Ltd for the year ended 31 March 20X1.**

(a) **Reconciliation of profit from operations to net cash from operating activities**

	£000
Profit before tax	
Adjustments for:	
	———
Cash generated by operations	
	———
Net cash from operating activities	
	———

(b) Rossington Ltd – Statement of cash flows for year ended 31 March 20X1

	£000
Net cash from operating activities	
Investing activities	
	——
Net cash used in investing activities	
Financing activities	
	——
Net cash from financing activities	
Net increase/(decrease) in cash and cash equivalents	
Cash and cash equivalents at beginning of year	
	——
Cash and cash equivalents at end of year	
	——

(c) Rossington Ltd – Statement of changes in equity for the year ended 31 March 20X1

	Share capital £000	Other reserves £000	Retained earnings £000	Total equity £000
Balance at 1 April 20X0				
Changes in equity for 20X1				
	——	——	——	——
Balance at 31 March 20X1				
	——	——	——	——

Workings

(W1) Changes in working capital

	£000 20X0	£000 20X1	Increase/ Decrease

(W2) Gain/loss on disposal of PPE

	£000

(W3) Purchase of PPE

	£000
Purchase of PPE	

(W4) Bank loans raised/redeemed

	£000 20X0	£000 20X1	Increase/ Decrease
Bank loans			

(W5) Share issue

	£000 20X0	£000 20X1	Increase/ Decrease
Share capital			
Share premium			
Total			

(W6) Dividends paid

	£000

9   RAINFORD LTD

DATA

You have been asked to prepare the statement of cash flows and the statement of changes in equity for Rainford Ltd for the year ended 30 September 20X3.

The statement of profit or loss and statement of financial position (with comparatives for the previous year) of Rainford Ltd for the year ended 30 September 20X3 were as follows:

Statement of profit or loss for the year ended 30 September 20X3

Continuing operations	£000
Revenue	1,397
Cost of sales	(1,110)
Gross profit	287
Gain on disposal of PPE	80
Operating expenses	(205)
Profit from operations	162
Dividends received and gain on investments	20
Finance costs	(40)
Profit before tax	142
Tax	(57)
Profit for the year from continuing operations	85

Statement of financial position as at 30 September

	20X3	20X2
ASSETS	£000	£000
Non-current assets		
Property, plant and equipment	1,280	940
Investments at cost	285	125
	1,565	1,065
Current assets		
Inventories	480	510
Trade and other receivables	270	380
Cash and cash equivalents	80	90
	830	980
Total assets	2,395	2,045

EQUITY AND LIABILITIES

Equity

Share capital	500	300
Share premium	150	85
Retained earnings	1,010	990
Total equity	**1,660**	**1,375**
Non-current liabilities		
Bank loans	300	25
Current liabilities		
Trade and other payables	353	555
Tax liabilities	57	50
Bank overdraft	25	40
	435	645
Total liabilities	735	670
Total equity and liabilities	2,395	2,045

Further information:

- The total depreciation charge for the year was £200,000.

- Property, plant and equipment with a carrying amount of £20,000 were sold in the year.

- All sales and purchases were on credit. Other expenses were paid in cash.

- A dividend of £65,000 was paid during the year.

(a) **Prepare a reconciliation of the profit from operations to net cash from operating activities (starting with profit before tax) for Rainford Ltd for the year ended 30 September 20X3.**

(b) **Prepare the statement of cash flows for Rainford Ltd for the year ended 30 September 20X3.**

(c) **Prepare the statement of changes in equity for Rainford Ltd for the year ended 30 September 20X3.**

(a)   **Rainford Ltd**

Reconciliation of profit from operations to net cash from operating activities

	£000
Profit before tax	
Adjustments for:	
	———
Cash generated by operations	
	———
Net cash from operating activities	
	———

(b)   **Rainford Ltd**

Statement of cash flows for year ended 30 September 20X3

	£000
Net cash from operating activities	
Investing activities	
	———
Net cash used in investing activities	
Financing activities	
	———
Net cash from financing activities	
Net increase/(decrease) in cash and cash equivalents	
Net cash and cash equivalents at beginning of year	
	———
Net cash and cash equivalents at end of year	
	———

Workings

(W1) Changes in working capital

	£000 20X3	£000 20X2	Increase/ Decrease
Inventories			
Trade receivables			
Trade payables			

(W2) Interest paid

	£000
Accrual b/f	
Profit or loss charge	
Accrual c/f	
Cash paid	

(W3) Proceeds on disposal of PPE

	£000
CA	
Gain on disposal	
Proceeds	

(W4) Tax paid

	£000
Accrual b/f	
Profit or loss charge	
Accrual c/f	
Cash paid	

(W5) Purchase of PPE

	£000
Balance b/f	
Disposals @ CA	
Depreciation charge	
Balance c/f	
Cash paid to purchase PPE	

(W6) Bank loans raised/redeemed

	£000 20X3	£000 20X2	Increase/ Decrease
Bank loans			

(W7)   Share issue

	£000 20X3	£000 20X2	Increase/ Decrease
Share capital			
Share premium			
Total			

(W8)   Retained earnings

	£000
Balance b/f	
Profit for the year	
Dividend for the year	
Balance c/f	

(W9)   Cash and equivalents

	£000 20X3	£000 20X2	Increase/ Decrease
Cash and equivalents			
Overdraft			
Net balance			

(c)   Rainford Ltd – Statement of changes in equity for the year ended 30 September 20X3

	Share capital	Share premium	Retained earnings	Total equity
	£000	£000	£000	£000
Balance at 1 October 20X2				
Changes in equity for the year				
	——	——	——	——
Balance at 30 September 20X3				
	——	——	——	——

REGULATORY AND CONCEPTUAL FRAMEWORKS AND DIFFERENT TYPES OF ORGANISATIONS

10 RECOGNITION

(a) What is the definition of an asset, liability and equity per the Conceptual Framework for Financial Reporting (the Framework)?

(b) What is the recognition criterion for these elements per the Framework?

11 OBJECTIVES

(a) What is the objective of the financial statements according to the Conceptual Framework for Financial Reporting?

(b) State two examples of EXTERNAL users of financial statements and describe their information requirements.

12 FUNDAMENTAL CHARACTERISTICS

(a) What are the two fundamental characteristics of useful financial information?

(b) What is the definition of an 'expense'?

13 CONCEPTUAL FRAMEWORK

(a) The Conceptual Framework for Financial Reporting identifies two fundamental qualitative characteristics of useful financial information: relevance and faithful representation.

Explain the two fundamental qualitative characteristics of useful financial information.

(b) The Conceptual Framework for Financial Reporting defines the five elements of the financial statements.

Define and explain liability and expense, two of the five elements, and include an example of each within your answer.

14 JACOB

Jacob has run a sweetshop business as a sole trader for many years, which has expanded considerably recently. Jacob is considering registering the business as a company, but is unsure what this means in terms of regulations that must be followed when preparing the financial statements.

Explain to Jacob the following:

(a) **which rules and legislation the company would need to follow**

(b) **the purpose of accounting standards.**

15   QUALITATIVE CHARACTERISTICS

Which one of these is not an 'enhancing' qualitative characteristic?

(i)   Comparability

(ii)   Timeliness

(iii)   Reliability

(iv)   Understandability

16   PUBLIC AND PRIVATE LIMITED COMPANIES

For each of the following statements, identify whether it is true or false:

	True	False
A private limited company is required to have a minimum of two members		
Both private and public limited companies are required to file their accounts on an annual basis		
Private limited companies may be exempt from an annual audit, but public companies cannot be exempt		
Public limited companies need to have at least £40,000 of issued share capital		

17   SOLE TRADER VS LIMITED COMPANIES

When considering sole traders and limited liability companies, which of the following statements are true?

(i)   The statement of profit or loss for a sole trader would show taxation as a business expense

(ii)   Companies have share capital whereas sole traders do not

(iii)   A sole trader is personally liable for any losses that the business might make

(iv)   Drawings would only appear in the financial statements of a sole trader

A   (i), (ii) and (iv)

B   (ii), (iii) and (iv)

C   (i), (ii) and (iii)

D   (i), (iii) and (iv)

18   AL

Al is thinking about setting up her own business, making and selling her own brand of chocolates ('the purple truffles'). She is unsure whether to operate her business as a sole trader or a limited company.

Write some brief notes to Al, which explain the key differences between operating as a sole trader and operating as a limited company.

INTERNATIONAL FINANCIAL REPORTING STANDARDS (WRITTEN QUESTIONS)

19   OAK PLC

The directors of Oak plc are reviewing the amounts recorded for property, plant and equipment in the financial statements and are unsure as to the treatment of certain items as they feel there are some inconsistencies.

Prepare brief notes for the directors of Oak plc to answer the following questions:

(a)   Why is land not depreciated?

(b)   When properties are revalued, why is there a difference in the accounting treatment for a revaluation gain and a revaluation loss?

(c)   Why does IAS 16 *Property, Plant and Equipment* permit a transfer within equity for the annual 'excess depreciation' charge arising as a result of revaluation of a building?

20   VICTORIA PLC

The directors of Victoria plc have recently undertaken some research into a new development project. Finance hasn't yet been obtained to undertake the development, although it is due to be received in the near future. The directors are aware of some rules governing the recognition of intangible assets, but are uncertain of the accounting treatment.

Prepare brief notes for the directors of Victoria plc to answer the following questions:

(a)   What is meant by an intangible asset according to IAS 38 *Intangible Assets*?

(b)   In addition to the availability of funds to complete, what other criteria would Victoria plc have to demonstrate about an intangible asset arising from development activities before it can be recognised as an intangible asset in the financial statements?

21   POPPY PLC

Poppy plc is about to acquire some assets under a lease agreement. The directors of Poppy plc would like to understand how to account for lease agreements.

Prepare brief notes for the directors of Poppy plc to cover the following:

(a)   What should be recognised in the financial statements at the start of a lease?

(b)   Whether a leased asset should be depreciated and if so over what period?

22   TODDY PLC

During the year ended 31 December 20X1, Toddy plc made some employees redundant. One of these is suing Toddy plc for wrongful dismissal. Legal advisors believe that Toddy plc will possibly lose. If they do lose, damages will be in the region of £200,000.

Prepare brief notes for the directors of Toddy plc to cover the following:

(a)   What criteria must exist before a provision can be recognised in the financial statements?

(b)   What is the correct accounting treatment of the legal case in the financial statements of Toddy plc for the year-ended 31 December 20X1?

(c)   Explain whether Toddy plc can recognise a provision in the financial statements for the year ended 31 December 20X1 for operating losses it expects to incur during January and February 20X2 as a consequence of deciding to close down a business activity.

23   ORMSKIRK LTD

Ormskirk Ltd manufactures and fits double glazed units such as windows and extensions to business and household premises.

The company now has the opportunity to purchase a brand name from a rival business, which has an excellent reputation, and which the directors of Ormskirk Ltd believe will attract new customers for their products.

If the brand was purchased, it would cost £100,000. The directors believe that the brand would have an estimated useful life of five years. The brand is not expected to have any realisable value at the end of its estimated useful life.

However, the directors have no experience of accounting for such items, although they are aware that there is an international financial reporting standard which deals with such items, IAS 38 *Intangible Assets*.

(a)   Prepare briefing notes for the Directors of Ormskirk Ltd that explain what an intangible asset is and how the brand name should be accounted for in the company financial statements based upon the information available.

(b)   Explain the accounting treatment if the directors are believe that the intangible asset has an indefinite useful life.

INTERNATIONAL FINANCIAL REPORTING STANDARDS (MULTIPLE CHOICE QUESTIONS)

24   FORMBY LTD AND OTHERS

Formby Ltd incurs significant research and development expenditure.

Statement: Development expenditure must be written off as an expense to profit or loss as it is incurred.

(a)   Is this statement true or false?

Statement: Research expenditure must be written off as an expense to profit or loss as it is incurred.

(b)   Is this statement true or false?

Melling Ltd values inventories in accordance with IAS 2 *Inventories*. At the year end of 30 June 20X5, it has the following information relating to inventories:

Product	Quantity units	Cost per unit £	Net realisable value £
A	100	20	25
B	200	15	13
C	300	12	10

(c)   What is the closing inventory valuation of Melling Ltd as at 30 June 20X5?

Choice	£
A	7,600
B	8,100
C	8,600
D	9,100

Product	Quantity units	Lower of cost or NRV £	Total value £
A			
B			
C			
			———
			———

Birkdale Ltd has an employee who was injured whilst operating a machine during the year ended 30 April 20X8. Upon inspection of the machine on 3 May 20X8, it was found that the machine was defective and not operating properly. On 15 May 20X8, the company received notice that the employee intends to sue the company for damages of £10,000 as a result of personal injury sustained from operating the machine. The company solicitor has advised that, if Birkdale Ltd is held responsible for the injury, the amount of £10,000 represents a reasonable estimate of damages that may be payable.

(d) (i) Does the claim received by the Birkdale Ltd represent an adjusting or non-adjusting event in accordance with IAS 10 *Events after the Reporting Period*?

(ii) Based upon the available information, should Birkdale Ltd include a provision in the financial statements for the claim of £10,000 in accordance with IAS 37 *Provisions, Contingent Assets and Contingent Liabilities*?

Answer:

(i)

(ii)

Kirkby Ltd is preparing the financial statements for the year ended 30 November 20X4, and the following is an extract of the trial balance at that date:

	£
Tax payable at 1 December 20X3	24,700
Tax paid during the year ended 30 November 20X4	25,100

The estimated corporation tax liability for the year ended 30 November 20X4 was £26,500.

The tax paid during the year was in full settlement of the amount due in respect of the year ended 30 November 20X3.

(e) (i) What is the amount of the operating activities cash flow that will be included in Kirkby Ltd's statement of cash flows for the year ended 30 November 20X4 in respect of taxation?

(ii) What is the tax charge that will be included in Kirkby Ltd's statement of profit or loss for the year ended 30 November 20X4?

Answer:

(i)

(ii)

Locke sells machines, and also offers installation and technical support services. The individual selling prices of each product are shown below.

Sale price of goods   £75
Installation   £25
One year service   £50

Company X bought a machine on 1 May 20X1, and was charged a reduced price of £100, including installation and one year's service.

Locke only offers discounts when customers purchase a package of products together.

(f) According to IFRS 15 *Revenue from Contracts with Customers*, how much should Locke record in revenue for the year ended 31 December 20X1? Workings should be rounded to the nearest £.

Answer:

£_____

IAS 2 INVENTORIES

25 CHESTNUT PLC

The financial controller of Chestnut plc is preparing the financial statements for the year ended 31 December 20X1 when the financial controller becomes aware that the valuation method for the inventory is incorrect resulting in the closing inventory being understated by £18,000.

What will be the impact of this error on the statement of profit or loss?

A   No impact

B   Gross profit and net profit are under-stated by £18,000

C   Gross profit and net profit are over-stated by £18,000

D   There is no impact on gross profit but net profit is under-stated by £18,000

26 FIFO

An inventory record card shows the following details:

April 1   100 units in inventory at a cost of £12/unit

April 5   120 units purchased at a cost of £14/unit

April 11   80 units sold

April 19   40 units purchased at a cost of £18/unit

April 27   90 units sold

If the company values its inventory on a periodic basis using FIFO, what value should the inventory be stated at in the financial statements according to IAS 2 *Inventories*?

A   £1,080

B   £1,246

C   £1,420

D   £1,460

27 WILKIE LTD

Wilkie Ltd is about to prepare its year-end Financial Statements, but is unsure how to value its inventory. The company maintains records as follows for the 3 wooden toys it manufactures:

Product	FIFO (cost)	LIFO (cost)	NRV
	£	£	£
Boat	47,600	42,000	53,740
Truck	17,975	16,482	16,800
Plane	25,800	34,500	29,450
	——	——	——
	91,375	92,982	99,990
	——	——	——

At what value should inventory be stated in Wilkie Ltd's financial statements according to IAS 2 *Inventories*?

A   £92,982

B   £84,282

C   £87,932

D   £90,200

28   SALT AND PEPPER LTD

Salt and pepper Ltd have recently performed an inventory count and have valued all of its four products in preparation for its financial year end.

	FIFO (cost)	LIFO (cost)	NRV
	£	£	£
Salt	15,450	11,300	9,800
Rock salt	23,055	24,500	27,060
Pepper	28,027	13,016	29,100
Thyme	5,100	5,700	8,200

At what value should inventory be stated in Salt and Pepper Ltd's financial statements according to IAS 2 *Inventories*?

A   £71,632

B   £54,516

C   £65,982

D   £50,971

IAS 7 STATEMENT OF CASH FLOWS

29   CASH FLOW

An increase in receivables will have a negative impact on the cash flow in the calculation of 'Net cash flows from financing activities'.

Is this statement true or false?

30   INDIRECT METHOD

When calculating 'cash generated from operations' using the indirect method, the annual depreciation expense should be deducted from 'profit from operations'?

Is this statement true or false?

31   DIRECT AND INDIRECT METHOD

If you calculate 'cash generated from operations' using the indirect method, the answer will be different than if you had used the direct method?

Is this statement true or false?

IAS 10 EVENTS AFTER THE REPORTING PERIOD

32   IAS 10

The following all occurred between the reporting date and the date the accounts are signed.

Which would be non-adjusting events per IAS 10?

(i)   The issue of new share capital

(ii)   The financial consequences of the loss of non-current assets as a result of a fire

(iii)   The acquisition of a subsidiary

(iv)   The liquidation of a credit customer

A   (i), (ii), (iii) and (iv)

B   (ii) and (iii) only

C   (i) and (iv) only

D   (i), (ii), and (iii) only

33   COLWYN LTD

Colwyn Ltd has a year end of 31 March 20X1. In June 20X1 Bay Ltd, a major credit customer went into liquidation and Colwyn's directors believe they will not be able to recover the £125,000 owed to them.

How should this item be treated in the financial statements of Colwyn Ltd for the year ended 31 March 20X1, in accordance with IAS 10 *Events after the Reporting Period?*

A   The irrecoverable debt should be disclosed as a note

B   The financial statements are not affected

C   The financial statements should be adjusted to reflect the irrecoverable debt

D   The financial statements should be adjusted to reflect the irrecoverable debt only if the going concern status of Colwyn Ltd is affected

34   EL GUARDO

El Guardo Ltd prepares its financial statements to 30 September each year. The following events took place between 30 September and 14 December, the date on which the financial statements were authorised for issue.

(i)   The company was sued for faulty goods. These goods were sold on 8 November.

(ii)   A customer who owed the company money at 30 September was declared bankrupt.

Which of the above is likely to be classified as an adjusting event according to IAS 10 *Events after the Reporting Period?*

A   (i) only

B   (ii) only

C   Both

D   Neither of them

---

35 FIRE

The following is an adjusting event according to IAS 10 *Events after the Reporting Period*:

A large fire destroyed one third of Green Ltd's inventory shortly after the year end (no impact on going concern).

Is this statement true or false?

36 EVENTS

Which of the following would be classified as a non-adjusting event according to IAS 10 *Events after the Reporting Period*?

1   Discovery of an irrecoverable debt of a major customer after the year end date

2   Declaration of a final dividend after the year end date

3   Fraud which has been discovered after the year end date

4   Fire which has destroyed the whole inventory of a company which happened after the year end date

A   1, 2, 3 and 4

B   1 only

C   1 and 2

D   2 and 4

IAS 16 PROPERTY, PLANT AND EQUIPMENT

37 LARCH PLC

Larch plc acquired a new machine from an overseas supplier. The machine cost £70,000 and delivery and installation costs were £5,000. Testing it amounted to £4,500 and training the employees on how to use the machine cost £800.

What should be the cost of the machine in the company's statement of financial position?

A   £70,000

B   £75,000

C   £79,500

D   £80,300

38 REVALUATION

A revaluation surplus will increase profit before tax in the statement of profit or loss.

Is this statement true or false?

39   ELLIOTT LTD

Elliott Ltd has recently invested some money.

Which of the following would be classified as capital expenditure?

1   Expenditure on the extension to the factory

2   Refurbishment costs to the main office

3   Repairs to the Warehouse roof

4   Cleaning its fleet of motor vehicles

A   1 only

B   1, 2 and 3

C   1, 2, 3 and 4

D   1 and 2 only

IFRS 16 LEASES

40   ASH PLC

On 1 July 20X1 Ash plc entered into a 4 year lease paying a deposit of £10,000 followed by 4 annual payments of £4,000. The present value of the annual payments is £8,500.

What amount should the right-of-use asset be recognised at in the statement of financial position when the least starts?

A   £8,500

B   £16,000

C   £26,000

D   £18,500

41   BECKI LTD

Becki Ltd signed a contract on 1 Jan 20X9 to lease a piece of machinery from Rob Ltd. The lease term is 16 years, and the asset is expected to have a useful economic life of 17 years.

The machine must be returned to Rob Ltd at the end of the lease term.

In accordance with IFRS 16 the asset should be depreciated over 17 years.

A   True

B   False

42 AXEL LTD

On 1 April 20X8 Axel Ltd acquires telephones for its sales team under a 1 year lease agreement. The term of the lease require an initial payment of £500, followed by two payments of £1,000 each on 30 September 20X8 and 31 March 20X9.

What amount should be recognised in the statement of profit and loss for the year ended 31 December 20X8 in respect of this transaction?

A   £2,000

B   £2,500

C   £1,875

D   £1,500

IAS 36 IMPAIRMENT OF ASSETS

43 FRANK LTD

Four assets owned by Frank Ltd were damaged by a freak accident on the last day of the year. They must now be reviewed for impairment, the following information is available:

	Value in use	Fair value less costs to sell	Carrying amount
	£	£	£
(i)	14,000	0	17,500
(ii)	23,500	27,000	24,000
(iii)	9,000	7,000	12,000
(iv)	0	6,500	5,000

What is the total value of the impairment loss (if any) that must be charged to the Statement of profit or loss in accordance with IAS 36 *Impairment of Assets*?

A   2,000

B   12,000

C   6,500

D   28,000

44   BOVEY LTD

Bovey Ltd holds two items of plant and equipment in its warehouse at the end of its accounting year, which are valued as follows:

Item	Carrying amount	Fair Value less costs to sell	Value in use
	£	£	£
(i)	13,000	3,200	9,000
(ii)	8,000	8,100	7,000

What amount should be charged to the Statement of profit or loss and other comprehensive income as an impairment according to IAS 36 *Impairment of Assets*?

A   £4,000

B   £5,000

C   £9,800

D   £10,800

45   LEMON LTD

Lemon Ltd has four assets which the directors consider may have become impaired.

Item	Carrying amount	Fair Value less costs to sell	Value in use
	£	£	£
1	20,000	24,000	28,000
2	16,000	18,000	11,600
3	14,000	7,600	14,400
4	18,000	8,600	10,400

What is the total value of these four assets which should be reflected in the statement of financial position according to IAS 36 *Impairment of Assets*?

A   £68,000

B   £47,800

C   £60,400

D   £64,400

46   IMPAIRMENT

An asset will be impaired according to IAS 36 *Impairment of Assets* if its carrying amount is lower than its recoverable amount.

Is this statement true or false?

47   ANNUAL TESTING

A building has been purchased and attributed a useful economic life of 50 years.

The building should be tested for impairment annually.

Is this statement true or false?

IAS 37 PROVISIONS, CONTINGENT LIABILITIES AND ASSETS

48 OBLIGATIONS

A present obligation arising from a past event that gives rise to a probable outflow of economic benefit that can be measured reliably is known as:

A   A provision

B   A contingent liability

49 TELVIN LTD

A former employee is claiming compensation of £35,000 from Telvin Ltd. The company's solicitors believe that the claim is unlikely to succeed. The legal costs relating to the claim have been estimated at £3,000 and will be incurred by the company regardless of whether or not the claim is successful.

How should the above information be treated in the financial statements of Telvin Ltd according to IAS 37 *Provisions, Contingent Assets and Contingent Liabilities*?

A   A provision should be made for £38,500

B   A provision should be made for £35,000 and the legal costs of £3,000 disclosed

C   A provision should be made for £3,000 and the claim for £35,000 disclosed

D   Nothing should be provided for but both items should be disclosed

50 KENYA LTD

Kenya Ltd is being sued by a customer due to the provision of faulty goods and will have to pay £1,000,000 if it loses the case. At its accounting year end lawyers advise the company that it is probable (i.e. more likely than not) that it will lose the case. Kenya Ltd has claimed for damages against the supplier of the goods, and lawyers have advised that it will probably succeed with an expected inflow of £800,000.

In accordance with IAS 37 *Provisions, Contingent Liabilities and Contingent Assets*, what accounting treatment should be followed?

A   Recognise a provision of £1,000,000 and an asset of £800,000 on the SFP

B   Recognise a provision of £1,000,000 on the SFP and disclose a contingent asset in the notes of £800,000

C   Disclose the outflow and inflow in the notes only

D   Disclose the outflow in the notes, ignore the inflow

51   CASEY LTD

Casey Ltd has two court cases currently in progress against them as a result of faulty goods supplied to customers.

The lawyers have advised the following:

Case I – Being sued for damages of £1,000,000 – 70% chance of successfully defending the case.

Case II – Being sued for damages of £375,000 – 60% chance of losing the case.

How much should be included in Casey Ltd's financial statements as a provision at the year end in line with IAS 37 *Provisions, Contingent Liabilities and Contingent Assets*?

A   £1,375,000

B   £1,000,000

C   £375,000

D   £225,000

IAS 38 INTANGIBLE ASSETS

52   GOODREP LTD

The directors of GoodRep Ltd started the business ten years ago. They believe that the GoodRep brand is well regarded and estimate that it is worth £3 million.

The directors of GoodRep Ltd can recognise an intangible asset in the statement of financial position for £3 million.

Is this statement true or false?

53   RESEARCH AND DEVELOPMENT

Which of the following correctly describes how research and development costs should be treated in accordance with IAS 38?

A   Research and development expenditure must be written off in the statement of profit or loss and other comprehensive income as incurred

B   Research and development expenditure should be capitalised as an intangible asset on the statement of financial position

C   Research expenditure should be capitalised as an intangible asset provided certain criteria are met; development expenditure should be written off to the statement of profit or loss and other comprehensive income

D   Development expenditure should be capitalised as an intangible asset provided certain criteria are met; research expenditure should be written off to the statement of profit or loss and other comprehensive income

IFRS 15 REVENUE FROM CONTRACTS WITH CUSTOMERS

54   NOTEBY LTD

Details of two of Noteby's transactions in the year ended 31 August 20X7 were as follows:

1   Noteby sold a machine to a customer, Pitt, on 28 August 20X7. Pitt is responsible for installation and operation of the machine following delivery.

2   Noteby sold a number of food mixers to Damon, on credit. Damon collected the food mixers from Noteby on 26 August 20X7. Damon has not yet paid for the goods purchased.

For which of the transactions should sales revenue be recognised?

A   1 only

B   2 only

C   Both 1 and 2

D   Neither 1 nor 2

CONSOLIDATED FINANCIAL STATEMENTS

55   BRYSON PLC

DATA

Bryson plc acquired 75% of the issued share capital of Stoppard Ltd on 1 April 20X0 for £6,720,000. At that date Stoppard Ltd had issued share capital of £4,800,000 and retained earnings of £672,000.

Extracts of the statements of financial position for the two companies one year later at 31 March 20X1 are as follows:

	Bryson £000	Stoppard £000
ASSETS		
Investment in Stoppard Ltd	6,720	
Non-current assets	11,280	3,670
Current assets	5,760	5,010
Total assets	23,760	8,680
EQUITY AND LIABILITIES		
Equity		
Share capital	7,200	4,800
Retained earnings	12,480	1,290
Total equity	19,680	6,090
Non-current liabilities	1,440	1,180
Current liabilities	2,640	1,410
Total liabilities	4,080	2,590
Total equity and liabilities	23,760	8,680

Additional data

- During the year Bryson sold goods to Stoppard for £960,000. None of the goods remained in Stoppard's inventory at the year end but Stoppard still owes half the amount payable to Bryson.

- The directors of Bryson plc have determined that goodwill has been impaired by £550,000.

- Land in Stoppard Ltd at 1 April 20X0 was carried at £650,000 but had a fair value of £1,100,000. This has not yet been reflected in the books of Stoppard Ltd.

Required:

Draft the consolidated statement of financial position for Bryson plc and its subsidiary undertaking as at 31 March 20X1.

Bryson – Consolidated statement of financial position as at 31 March 20X1

	£000
ASSETS	
	———
Total assets	
	———
EQUITY AND LIABILITIES	
Equity	
	———
Total equity	
	———
Non-current liabilities	
Current liabilities	
	———
Total liabilities	
	———
Total equity and liabilities	
	———

Workings

(W1) Calculate goodwill

Goodwill	£000
Goodwill in SFP	

(W2) Calculate NCI

Non-controlling Interest	£000
Total	

(W3) Calculate retained earnings

Retained earnings	£000
Total	

(W4) Current assets

	£000
Total	

(W5) Current liabilities

	£000
Total	

56 SUGAR PLC

DATA

Sugar plc acquired 80% of the issued share capital of Brady Ltd on 1 April 20X0.

Extracts from their statements of profit or loss for the year ended 31 March 20X1 are shown below:

	Sugar plc £000	Brady Ltd £000
Revenue	97,900	44,600
Cost of sales	(58,800)	(17,500)
Gross profit	39,100	27,100
Other income – dividend from Brady Ltd	4,000	–
Distribution costs and administrative expenses	(6,000)	(3,800)
Profit before tax	37,100	23,300

Additional data

Just before the year end Brady sold goods which had cost £240,000 to Sugar plc for £336,000. These goods all still remain in Sugar's inventory at the year end.

Required:

Draft the consolidated statement of profit or loss for Sugar plc and its subsidiary undertaking up to and including the profit before tax line for the year ended 31 March 20X1.

Sugar plc – Consolidated statement of profit or loss for the year ended 31 March 20X1

	£000
Continuing operations	
	———
	———
Profit before tax	
	———

Workings

(W1) Revenue

	£000
Total	

(W2) COS

	£000
Total	

(W3) Provision for unrealised profits

	£000

57   SPENCER PLC

DATA

Spencer plc acquired 1,300,000 ordinary shares in Marks Ltd on 1 September 20X0 for £5,400,000. At that date Marks Ltd had issued share capital of £2,000,000 and retained earnings of £5,200,000.

Extracts of the statements of financial position for the two companies at 31 March 20X1 are as follows:

	Spencer plc £000	Marks Ltd £000
ASSETS		
Investment in Marks Ltd	5,400	
Non-current assets	12,576	7,490
Current assets	5,136	2,140
Total assets	23,112	9,630
Equity		
Share capital £1 ordinary shares	5,000	2,000
Retained earnings	13,840	5,850
Total equity	18,840	7,850
Non-current liabilities	2,880	1,200
Current liabilities	1,392	580
Total liabilities	4,272	1,780
Total equity and liabilities	23,112	9,630

Additional data

- During March, Spencer sold some goods to Marks for £420,000 at a profit margin of 20%. Two thirds of the goods had been sold by Marks by the year end.

- The balance from the intercompany sales remains unpaid at the end of the year and is included within the current assets of Spencer plc and in the current liabilities of Marks Ltd.

Required:

Draft the consolidated statement of financial position for Spencer plc and its subsidiary undertaking as at 31 March 20X1.

Spencer plc – Consolidated statement of financial position as at 31 March 20X1

	£000
ASSETS	
	———
Total assets	
	———
EQUITY AND LIABILITIES	
Equity	
	———
Total equity	
	———
Non-current liabilities	
Current liabilities	
	———
Total liabilities	
	———
Total equity and liabilities	
	———

Workings

(W1) Calculate goodwill

Goodwill	£000
Goodwill in SFP	

(W2) Calculate NCI

Non-controlling interest	£000
Total	

(W3) Calculate retained earnings

Retained earnings	£000
Total	

(W4) Current assets

	£000
Total	

(W5) Current liabilities

	£000
Total	

(W6) Unrealised profit

	£000	%

58 MITCHELL PLC

DATA

Mitchell plc acquired 65% of the issued share capital of Camper Ltd on 1 April 20X0.

Extracts from their statements of profit or loss for the year ended 31 March 20X1 are shown below:

	Mitchell plc	Camper Ltd
	£000	£000
Revenue	86,720	22,920
Cost of sales	(51,340)	(9,690)
Gross profit	35,380	13,230
Distribution costs	(7,620)	(1,280)
Administrative expenses	(8,430)	(950)
Profit from operating activities	19,330	11,000
Investment income	8,000	–
Profit before tax	27,330	11,000
Taxation	(7,500)	(3,080)
Profit after tax	19,830	7,920

Additional data

During the year Mitchell plc sold goods which had cost £850,000 to Camper Ltd for £1,200,000. None of these goods remain in inventory at the end of the year.

Camper paid a dividend during the year of £10,000,000. Mitchell plc has included its share within investment income.

(a) **Draft the consolidated statement of profit or loss for Mitchell plc and its subsidiary undertaking up to and including the profit after tax line for the year ended 31 March 20X1.**

(b) **Calculate the figures attributable to non-controlling interest and equity holders of the parent that would be recorded in the consolidated statement of profit or loss for the year ended 31 March 20X1.**

Mitchell plc – Consolidated statement of profit or loss for the year ended 31 March 20X1

	£000
Continuing operations	
	————
Gross profit	
	————
Profit from operating activities	
	————
Profit before tax	
	————
Profit after tax	

Workings

(W1) Revenue

	£000
Total	

(W2) COS

	£000
Total	

59   TIPPERS PLC

DATA

Tippers plc acquired 70% of the issued share capital of Holmes Ltd on 1 April 20X0 for £1,800,000. At that date Holmes Ltd had issued share capital of £1,000,000 and retained earnings of £140,000.

Extracts of the statements of financial position for the two companies one year later at 31 March 20X1 are as follows:

	Tippers plc	Holmes Ltd
	£000	£000
ASSETS		
Investment in Holmes Ltd	1,800	
Non-current assets	3,800	2,530
Current assets	4,000	1,690
Total assets	9,600	4,220
EQUITY AND LIABILITIES		
Equity		
Share capital	3,000	1,000
Retained earnings	5,200	720
Total equity	8,200	1,720
Non-current liabilities	750	1,980
Current liabilities	650	520
Total liabilities	1,400	2,500
Total equity and liabilities	9,600	4,220

Additional data

- Included within the current assets of Tippers plc and in the current liabilities of Holmes Ltd is an inter-company transaction for £200,000 that took place in early March 20X1.

- Land in Holmes Ltd at 1 April 20X0 was carried at £800,000 but had a fair value of £1,200,000. This has not yet been reflected in the books of Holmes Ltd.

- Goodwill has suffered an impairment loss of 12%.

Draft the consolidated statement of financial position for Tippers plc and its subsidiary undertaking as at 31 March 20X1.

Your calculations should work to the nearest £000.

Tippers plc – Consolidated statement of financial position as at 31 March 20X1

	£000
ASSETS	
	————
Total assets	
	————
EQUITY AND LIABILITIES	
Equity	
	————
Total equity	
	————
Non-current liabilities	
Current liabilities	
	————
Total liabilities	
	————
Total equity and liabilities	
	————

Workings

(W1) Calculate goodwill

Goodwill	£000
Goodwill in SFP	

(W2) Calculate NCI

Non-controlling interest	£000
Total	

(W3) Calculate retained earnings

Retained earnings	£000
Total	

(W4) Current assets

	£000
Total	

(W5) Current liabilities

	£000
Total	

60   LUCY PLC

DATA

Lucy plc acquired 90% of the issued share capital of Colin Ltd on 1 April 20X0.

Extracts from their statements of profit or loss for the year ended 31 March 20X1 are shown below:

	Lucy plc	Colin Ltd
	£	£
Revenue	940,620	535,970
Cost of sales	(781,900)	(387,980)
Gross profit	158,720	147,990
Other income – dividend from Colin Ltd	18,000	–
Distribution costs and administrative expenses	(24,320)	(15,640)
Profit before tax	152,400	132,350

Additional data

During the year Colin Ltd sold goods which had cost £36,000 to Lucy plc for £50,000. None of these goods remained in inventory at the end of the year.

Draft the consolidated statement of profit or loss for Lucy plc and its subsidiary for the year ended 31 March 20X1.

Lucy plc – Consolidated statement of profit or loss for the year ended 31 March 20X1

	£
Continuing operations	
Gross profit	
Profit before tax	
Attributable to:	
Equity holders of Lucy plc	
Non-controlling interest	

Workings

(W1) Revenue

	£
Total	

(W2) COS

	£
Total	

61 TROY PLC

DATA

Troy plc acquired 4,000,000 of Sherman Ltd's shares on 1 July 20X8 for £5,500,000. At that date Sherman Ltd had issued share capital of £5,000,000 (£1 nominal value) and retained earnings of £720,000.

Extracts of the statements of financial position for the two companies one year later at 30 June 20X9 are as follows:

	Troy plc £000	Sherman Ltd £000
ASSETS		
Investment in Sherman Ltd	6,000	
Non-current assets	17,200	5,000
Current assets	4,480	2,860
Total assets	27,680	7,860
EQUITY AND LIABILITIES		
Equity		
Share capital	10,000	5,000
Retained earnings	5,090	1,080
Total equity	15,090	6,080
Non-current liabilities	8,000	500
Current liabilities	4,590	1,280
Total liabilities	12,590	1,780
Total equity and liabilities	27,680	7,860

Additional data

- The non-current liabilities included in Sherman Ltd's Statement of Financial Position are an intercompany loan that Troy plc gave shortly after acquisition. The corresponding amount is included within 'Investment in Sherman Ltd' in Troy's statements.

- Consolidated goodwill has been impaired by £100,000 since acquisition.

Draft the consolidated statement of financial position for Troy plc and its subsidiary undertaking as at 30 June 20X9.

Troy plc – Consolidated statement of financial position as at 30 June 20X9.

	£000
ASSETS	
	———
Total assets	
	———
EQUITY AND LIABILITIES	
Equity	
	———
Total equity	
	———
Non-current liabilities	
Current liabilities	
	———
Total liabilities	
	———
Total equity and liabilities	
	———

Workings

(W1) Calculate goodwill

Goodwill	£000
Goodwill in SFP	

(W2) Calculate NCI

Non-controlling interest	£000
Total	

(W3) Calculate retained earnings

Retained earnings	£000
Total	

(W4) Current assets

	£000
Total	

(W5) Current liabilities

	£000
Total	

(W6) Non-current liabilities

	£000
Total	

62   CACTUS PLC

DATA

Cactus plc acquired 75% of the issued share capital of Shore Ltd on 1 April 20X8.

Extracts from their statements of profit or loss for the year ended 31 March 20X9 are shown below:

	Cactus plc	Shore Ltd
	£000	£000
Revenue	20,500	15,200
Cost of sales	(11,200)	(8,200)
Gross profit	9,300	7,000
Other income – dividend from Shore Ltd	700	–
Distribution costs and administrative expenses	(6,900)	(4,800)
Profit before tax	3,100	2,200
Income tax expense	(620)	(440)
Profit for the year	2,480	1,760

Additional data

(i)   During the year Shore Ltd sold goods which had cost £500,000 to Cactus plc for £800,000. One quarter of these goods still remain in inventory at the end of the year.

(ii)   Consolidated goodwill has been impaired by £50,000 in the year

Draft the consolidated statement of profit or loss for Cactus plc and its subsidiary undertaking for the year ended 31 March 20X9.

Cactus plc – Consolidated statement of profit or loss for the year ended 31 March 20X9

	£000
Continuing operations	
Gross profit	
Profit before tax	
Income tax expense	
Profit for the year	
Attributable to:	
Equity holders of Cactus plc	
Non-controlling interest	

Workings

(W1) Revenue

	£000
Total	

(W2) COS

	£000
Total	

(W3) Provision for unrealised profits

	£000

(W4) Non-controlling interest

	£000
Total	

63 JACK PLC

DATA

Jack plc acquired 70% of the issued share capital of Jill Ltd on 1 April 20X8 for £5,600,000. At that date Jill Ltd had issued share capital of £4,000,000 and retained earnings of £560,000.

Extracts of the statements of financial position for the two companies one year later at 31 March 20X9 are as follows:

	Jack plc £000	Jill Ltd £000
ASSETS		
Investment in Jill Ltd	5,600	
Non-current assets	9,400	3,060
Current assets	4,800	4,180
Total assets	19,800	7,240
EQUITY AND LIABILITIES		
Equity		
Share capital	6,000	4,000
Retained earnings	10,400	1,080
Total equity	16,400	5,080
Non-current liabilities	1,200	960
Current liabilities	2,200	1,200
Total liabilities	3,400	2,160
Total equity and liabilities	19,800	7,240

Additional data

- Included within the current assets of Jill plc and the current liabilities of Jack Ltd is an inter-company balance of £400,000, relating to a sale that took place in early March 20X9. The sale was made at a margin of 30% and a quarter of the goods remain in inventory at the year end.

- Goodwill has been impaired by £250,000 since acquisition.

Draft the consolidated statement of financial position for Jack plc and its subsidiary undertaking as at 31 March 20X9.

Jack plc – Consolidated statement of financial position as at 31 March 20X9

	£000
ASSETS	
	————
Total assets	
	————
EQUITY AND LIABILITIES	
Equity	
	————
Total equity	
	————
Non-current liabilities	
Current liabilities	
	————
Total liabilities	
	————
Total equity and liabilities	
	————

Workings

(W1) Calculate goodwill

Goodwill	£000
Goodwill in SFP	

(W2) Calculate NCI

Non-controlling Interest	£000
Total	

(W3) Calculate retained earnings

Retained earnings	£000
Total	

(W4) Current assets

	£000
Total	

(W5) Current liabilities

	£000
Total	

(W6) Unrealised profit

	£000	%

64   KEN PLC

DATA

Ken plc acquired 90% of the issued share capital of Barbie Ltd on 1 April 20X8.

Extracts from their statement of profit or loss for the year ended 31 March 20X9 are shown below:

	Ken plc	Barbie Ltd
	£000	£000
Revenue	20,400	9,300
Cost of sales	(12,100)	(3,650)
Gross Profit	8,300	5,650
Other income – dividend from Barbie Ltd	900	–
Distribution costs and administrative expenses	(1,250)	(800)
Profit before tax	7,950	4,850

Additional data

During the year Barbie Ltd sold goods which had cost £50,000 to Ken plc for £240,000. Half of these goods still remain in inventory at the end of the year.

Draft the consolidated statement of profit or loss for Ken plc and its subsidiary undertaking up to and including the profit before tax line for the year ended 31 March 20X9.

Ken plc – Consolidated statement of profit or loss for the year ended 31 March 20X9.

	£000
Continuing operations	
Profit before tax	

Workings

(W1) Revenue

	£000
Total	

(W2) COS

	£000
Total	

(W3) Provision for unrealised profits

	£000

65 NORTHWOOD PLC

DATA

Northwood plc acquired 75% of the issued share capital and voting rights of Southdean Ltd on 1 January 20X6 for £900,000. At that date, Southdean Ltd had issued share capital of £400,000, share premium account of £200,000 and retained earnings of £500,000.

Calculate the figures for goodwill and non-controlling interest at the date of acquisition of Southdean Ltd by Northwood plc.

Goodwill at date of acquisition	
	£000
	———
Goodwill	
	———

Non-controlling interest at date of acquisition	
	£000
	——
NCI at acquisition	
	——

66 TOWERHILL GROUP

Towerhill plc acquired 75% of the issued share capital and voting rights of Westvale Ltd on 1 January 20X5. Extracts from both companies statements of profit or loss for the year ended 31 December 20X5, plus additional information is as follows:

Statements of profit of loss for the year ended 31 December 20X5

	Towerhill plc	Westvale Ltd
	£000	£000
Continuing operations		
Revenue	500	450
Cost of sales	(275)	(220)
	——	——
Gross profit	225	230
Other income	80	40
Distribution costs	(60)	(45)
Administrative expenses	(30)	(35)
	——	——
Profit from operations	215	190
Finance costs	(20)	(15)
	——	——
Profit before tax	195	175
Tax	(40)	(35)
	——	——
Profit for the year from continuing operations	155	140
	——	——

Additional information:

- During the year, Towerhill plc purchased goods from a supplier at a cost of £20,000 and sold the goods to Westvale Ltd for £24,000. At the end of the year, one quarter of these goods remained within the inventory of Westvale Ltd.

- The other income of Towerhill plc includes a dividend received of £10,000 from Westvale Ltd.

Prepare the consolidated statement of profit or loss for Towerhill plc and its subsidiary for the year ended 31 December 20X5.

Consolidated statement of profit or loss for the year ended 31 December 20X5.

	Towerhill plc £000
Continuing operations	
Revenue	
Cost of sales	
Gross profit	
Other income	
Distribution costs	
Administrative expenses	
Profit from operations	
Finance costs	
Profit before tax	
Tax	
Profit for the year from continuing operations	
Attributable to:	
Equity holders of the parent	
Non-controlling interest	

Workings

(W1) Revenue

	£000
T plc	
W Ltd	
Interco sale	

(W2) Cost of sales

	£000
T plc	
W Ltd	
Interco purchase	
PUP adjust	
	472

(W3) PUP working

	£000	
Selling price		
Cost of goods sold		
Profit		
PUP adjust		

(W4) Other income

	£000
T plc	
W Ltd	
Divi from W Ltd	
	———
	———

(W5) Distribution costs

	£000
T plc	
W Ltd	
	———
	———

(W6) Administrative expenses

	£000
T plc	
W Ltd	
	———
	———

(W7) Finance costs

	£000
T plc	
W Ltd	
	———
	———

(W8) Tax expense

	£000
T plc	
W Ltd	
	———
	———

ANALYSIS AND INTERPRETATION OF FINANCIAL STATEMENTS (FORMULAS AND CALCULATIONS)

67 PAREK LTD

DATA

You have been asked to calculate ratios for Parek Ltd in respect of its financial statements for the year ending 31 March 20X1 to assist your manager with the analysis of the company.

Parek Ltd's statement of profit or loss and other comprehensive income and statement of financial position are set out below.

Parek Ltd – Statement of profit or loss and other comprehensive income for the year ended 31 March 20X1

	20X1
	£000
Revenue	39,680
Cost of sales	(20,435)
	———
Gross profit	19,245
Distribution costs	(10,880)
Administrative expenses	(5,190)
	———
Profit from operations	3,175
Finance costs	(595)
	———
Profit before tax	2,580
Tax	(1,585)
	———
Profit for the period	995
	———

Parek Ltd – Statement of financial position as at 31 March 20X1

	20X1
	£000
ASSETS	
Non-current assets	
Property, plant and equipment	29,120
	———
Current assets	
Inventories	2,016
Trade receivables	3,712
Cash and cash equivalents	2,942
	———
	8,670
	———
Total assets	37,790
	———

EQUITY AND LIABILITIES
Equity

Share capital £1 ordinary shares	20,000
Retained earnings	11,530
	———
Total equity	31,530
	———
Non-current liabilities	
Bank loans	3,000
	———
	3,000
	———
Current liabilities	
Trade payables	1,675
Tax liabilities	1,585
	———
	3,260
	———
Total liabilities	6,260
	———
Total equity and liabilities	37,790
	———

(a)   State the formulas that are used to calculate each of the following ratios:

   (i)   Gross profit percentage

   (ii)   Operating profit percentage

   (iii)   Return on capital employed

   (iv)   Current ratio

   (v)   Trade receivable collection period

   (vi)   Trade payables payment period

   (vii)   Gearing ratio.

(b)   Calculate the above ratios.

(a) and (b) Formulas and calculation of the ratios

	20X1	
Gross profit percentage		
Operating profit percentage		
Return on capital employed		

Current ratio		
Trade receivable collection period		
Trade payables payment period		
Gearing ratio		

68 REGENCY LTD

DATA

You have been asked to calculate ratios for Regency Ltd in respect of its financial statements for the year ending 31 March 20X1 to assist your manager with a financial analysis of the company.

Regency Ltd's statement of profit or loss and other comprehensive income and statement of financial position are set out below.

Regency Ltd – Statement of profit or loss and other comprehensive income for the year ended 31 March 20X1

	20X1
	£000
Revenue	37,920
Cost of sales	(18,696)
	————
Gross profit	19,224
Distribution costs	(9,220)
Administrative expenses	(4,782)
	————
Profit from operations	5,222
Finance costs	(529)
	————
Profit before tax	4,693
Tax	(1,313)
	————
Profit for the period	3,380
	————

Regency Ltd – Statement of financial position as at 31 March 20X1

	20X1
	£000
ASSETS	
Non-current assets	
Property, plant and equipment	24,600
Current assets	
Inventories	1,872
Trade receivables	3,795
Cash and cash equivalents	2,185
	7,852
Total assets	32,452
Equity	
Share capital	10,000
Retained earnings	12,626
Total equity	22,626
Non-current liabilities	
Bank loans	5,000
	5,000
Current liabilities	
Trade payables	3,513
Tax liabilities	1,313
	4,826
Total liabilities	9,826
Total equity and liabilities	32,452

(a) **State the formulas that are used to calculate each of the following ratios:**

   (i)   Gross profit percentage

   (ii)   Expenses/revenue percentage

   (iii)   Return on shareholders' funds

   (iv)   Current ratio

   (v)   Acid test ratio

   (vi)   Trade receivable collection period

   (vii)   Trade payable payment period

   (viii) Gearing ratio.

(b) **Calculate the above ratios.**

(a) and (b) Formulas and calculation of the ratios

	20X1	
Gross profit percentage	**Working £000**	**Answer**
Expenses/revenue percentage		
Return on shareholders' funds		
Current ratio		
Acid test ratio		
Trade receivable collection period		
Trade payables payment period		
Gearing ratio		

69 ARCTIC FOX LTD

DATA

You have been asked to calculate ratios for Arctic Fox Ltd in respect of its financial statements for the year ending 31 March 20X1 to assist your manager with a financial analysis of the company.

Arctic Fox Ltd's statement of profit or loss and other comprehensive income and statement of financial position are set out below.

Arctic Fox Ltd – Statement of profit or loss and other comprehensive income for the year ended 31 March 20X1

	20X1
	£000
Revenue	20,500
Cost of sales	(18,000)
	––––––
Gross profit	2,500
Distribution costs	(300)
Administrative expenses	(210)
	––––––
Profit from operations	1,990
Finance costs	(590)
	––––––
Profit before tax	1,400
Tax	(400)
	––––––
Profit for the period	1,000
	––––––

Arctic Fox Ltd – Statement of financial position as at 31 March 20X1

	20X1
	£000
ASSETS	
Non-current assets	
Property, plant and equipment	5,800
	––––––
Current assets	
Inventories	3,600
Trade receivables	2,400
Cash and cash equivalents	1,300
	––––––
	7,300
	––––––
Total assets	13,100
	––––––

EQUITY AND LIABILITIES

Equity

Share capital	2,000
Retained earnings	800
Total equity	2,800
Non-current liabilities	
Bank loans	6,300
	6,300
Current liabilities	
Trade payables	3,800
Tax liabilities	200
	4,000
Total liabilities	10,300
Total equity and liabilities	13,100

(a) **State the formulas that are used to calculate each of the following ratios:**

   (i)   Gross profit percentage

   (ii)   Asset turnover (net assets)

   (iii) Return on capital employed

   (iv)   Current ratio

   (v)   Acid test ratio

   (vi)   Trade payable collection period

   (vii) Inventory holding period (days)

   (viii) Gearing ratio

   (ix)   Interest cover.

(b) **Calculate the above ratios.**

(a) and (b) Formulas and calculation of the ratios

	20X1	
Gross profit percentage	**Working £000**	**Answer**
Asset turnover (net assets)		
Return on capital employed		
Current ratio		
Acid test ratio		
Trade payable collection period		
Inventory holding period (days)		
Gearing ratio		
Interest cover		

70   SHIELD LTD

DATA

You have been asked you to calculate ratios for Shield Ltd in respect of its financial statements for the year ending 31 July 20X9 to assist your manager with a financial analysis of the company.

Shield Ltd's statement of profit or loss and other comprehensive income and statement of financial position are set out below.

Shield Ltd – Statement of profit or loss and other comprehensive income for the year ended 31 July 20X9

	20X9
	£000
Revenue	45,700
Cost of sales	(29,300)
Gross profit	16,400
Distribution costs	(5,720)
Administrative expenses	(4,424)
Profit from operations	6,256
Finance costs	(1,233)
Profit before tax	5,023
Tax	(2,129)
Profit for the period	2,894

Shield Ltd – Statement of financial position as at 31 July 20X9

	20X9
	£000
ASSETS	
Non-current assets	
Property, plant and equipment	35,700
Current assets	
Inventories	2,220
Trade receivables	3,970
Cash and cash equivalents	820
	7,010
Total assets	42,710

Equity

Share capital	15,000
Retained earnings	12,312
	———
Total equity	27,312
	———
Non-current liabilities	
Bank loans	6,000
	———
	6,000
	———
Current liabilities	
Trade payables	7,269
Tax liabilities	2,129
	———
	9,398
	———
Total liabilities	15,398
	———
Total equity and liabilities	42,710
	———

(a)   **State the formulas that are used to calculate each of the following ratios:**

   (i)   Gross profit percentage

   (ii)   Operating profit percentage

   (iii)   Current ratio

   (iv)   Acid test ratio

   (v)   Trade receivable collection period

   (vi)   Inventory turnover

   (vii)   Gearing ratio.

(b)   **Calculate the above ratios.**

(a) and (b) Formulas and calculation of the ratios

	20X1	
Gross profit percentage	**Working £000**	**Answer**
Operating profit percentage		
Current ratio		
Acid test ratio		
Trade receivable collection period		
Inventory turnover		
Gearing ratio		

71   SUGAR AND SPICE LTD

DATA

You have been asked to calculate ratios for Sugar & Spice Ltd in respect of its financial statements for the year ending 31 March 20X9 to assist your manager with a financial analysis of the company.

Sugar & Spice Ltd's statement of profit or loss and other comprehensive income and statement of financial position are set out below.

Sugar & Spice Ltd – Statement of profit or loss and other comprehensive income for the year ended 31 March 20X9

	20X9
	£000
Revenue	74,400
Cost of sales	(38,316)
Gross profit	36,084
Distribution costs	(20,400)
Administrative expenses	(9,732)
Profit from operations	5,952
Finance costs	(1,116)
Profit before tax	4,836
Tax	(2,976)
Profit for the period	**1,860**

Sugar & Spice Ltd – Statement of financial position as at the 31 March 20X9

	20X9
	£000
ASSETS	
Non-current assets	
Property, plant and equipment	54,600
Current assets	
Inventories	3,780
Trade receivables	6,960
Cash and cash equivalents	5,520
	16,260
Total assets	**70,860**

EQUITY AND LIABILITIES

Equity

Share capital	36,000
Retained earnings	21,636
Total equity	57,636

Non-current liabilities

Bank loans	6,000
	6,000

Current liabilities

Trade payables	4,248
Tax liabilities	2,976
	7,224
Total liabilities	13,224
Total equity and liabilities	70,860

(a)   State the formulas that are used to calculate each of the following ratios:

(i)   Asset turnover (net assets)

(ii)   Operating profit percentage

(iii)   Return on capital employed

(iv)   Current ratio

(v)   Acid test ratio

(vi)   Trade receivable collection period

(vii) Inventory holding period (days)

(viii) Gearing ratio.

(b)   Calculate the above ratios.

(a) and (b) Formulas and calculation of the ratios

	20X1	
Asset turnover	**Working £000**	**Answer**
Operating profit percentage		
Return on capital employed		
Current ratio		
Acid test ratio		
Trade receivable collection period		
Inventory holding period (days)		
Gearing ratio		

72   HIGHTOWN LTD

DATA

You have been given the financial statements of Hightown Ltd for the year ended 30 April 20X7. You are now required to prepare financial ratios to assist your manager with an analysis of that company.

Statement of profit or loss for the year ended 30 April 20X7

	£000
Continuing operations	
Revenue	23,750
Cost of sales	(12,231)
Gross profit	11,519
Distribution costs	(3,800)
Administrative expenses	(2,375)
Profit from operations	5,344
Finance costs	(60)
Profit before tax	5,284
Tax	(1,058)
Profit for the year from continuing operations	4,226

Statement of financial position as at 30 April 20X7

ASSETS	£000
Non-current assets	
Property, plant and equipment	9,325
Current assets	
Inventories	2,446
Trade and other receivables	3,669
Cash and cash equivalents	100
	6,215
Total assets	15,540

EQUITY AND LIABILITIES

Equity

Ordinary share capital @ £1 shares	500
Retained earnings	8,500
Total equity	**9,000**
Non-current liabilities	
Bank loans	1,000
Current liabilities	
Trade and other payables	4,482
Tax liabilities	1,058
	5,540
Total liabilities	6,540
Total equity and liabilities	15,540

(a)   State the formulas that are used to calculate each of the following ratios:

   (i)   Return on capital employed

   (ii)   Interest cover

   (iii)   Current ratio

   (vi)   Operating profit percentage

   (v)   Inventory holding period (days).

(b)   Calculate each of the above ratios to one decimal place.

	Formula	Calculation
Return on capital employed		
Interest cover		
Current ratio		
Operating profit percentage		
Inventory holding period (days)		

ANALYSIS AND INTERPRETATION OF FINANCIAL STATEMENTS (WRITTEN ELEMENT)

73   CHILLED LTD

Michael Davies has just been appointed as a non-executive director to the board of Chilled Ltd and he is trying to assess how the company has performed in the last couple of years. He has asked you to assist him in determining the level of profitability and risk of the company. You have computed the following ratios in respect of Chilled Ltd's financial statements for the last two years to assist you in your analysis.

	20X1	20X0
Gross profit percentage	38.0%	32.0%
Operating profit percentage	5.5%	7.2%
Return on capital employed	8.0%	12.4%
Gearing	28.6%	21.5%
Interest cover	3.2 times	6.1 times

Prepare a report to Michael that includes:

(a)   **a comment on the relative performance of the company for the two years based on the ratios calculated and what this tells you about the company**

(b)   **what Michael should be advising the company in his role as a non-executive director.**

74   WESTELLA LTD

Claire Jones is a shareholder in Westella Ltd. She wishes to assess the level of profitability and the level of risk of maintaining her investment in the company. You have computed the following ratios in respect of Westella Ltd's financial statements for the last two years to assist you in your analysis.

	20X1	20X0
Gross profit percentage	47.50%	45.00%
Operating profit percentage	8.50%	12.00%
Gearing	43.61%	34.67%
Quick ratio	0.9:1	1.2:1
Return on equity/shareholders' funds	8.40%	11.80%

Prepare a report to Claire that includes:

(a)   **a comment on the relative performance of the company for the two years based on the ratios calculated and what this tells you about the company**

(b)   **advice, with reasons based on the ratios you have calculated, on whether or not Claire should keep investing in Westella Ltd.**

75   CALIFORNIA LTD

Daisy Duke is considering buying shares in California Ltd and has asked you to assist her in determining the level of profitability and risk of the company. You have computed the following ratios in respect of California Ltd's financial statements for the last two years to assist you in your analysis.

	20X9	20X8
Gross profit percentage	35.0%	29.0%
Return on equity/shareholders' funds	15.2%	12.3%
Inventory turnover	7.2	6.7
Interest cover	3.9 times	1.8 times

Prepare a report to Daisy that includes:

(a)   a comment on the relative performance of the company for the two years based on the ratios calculated and what this tells you about the company

(b)   advice, with reasons based on the ratios you have calculated, on whether or not Daisy should invest.

76   JOHN LTD

Tina Campbell is considering buying shares in John Ltd and has asked you to assist her in determining the level of profitability and risk of the company. You have computed the following ratios in respect of John Ltd's financial statements for the last two years to assist you in your analysis.

	20X1	20X0
Operating profit percentage	3.8%	6.4%
Return on capital employed	7.7%	8.7%
Trade receivables collection period	61 days	47 days
Trade payables payment period	18 days	20 days
Gearing	46.7%	12.3%

Prepare a report to Tina that includes:

(a)   a comment on the relative performance of the company for the two years based on the ratios calculated and what this tells you about the company

(b)   advice, with reasons based on the ratios you have calculated, on whether or not Tina should invest.

77   CHAN LTD

You are employed by Chan Ltd and have been asked to review the working capital management of the company for the last two years.

You have calculated the following key ratios based upon information extracted from the financial statements for the years ended 31 December 20X9 and 20X8:

	20X9	20X8
Inventory holding period	26 days	30 days
Trade receivables collection period	40 days	45 days
Trade payables payment period	35 days	30 days
Working capital cycle	31 days	45 days

Prepare notes which include:

(a)   **Comment on the working capital management of Chan Ltd for the two years ended 31 December 20X9, giving possible reasons for the change in financial performance from 20X8 to 20X9.**

(b)   **Explain why financial ratios calculated using historic financial information may not always be a good basis for predicting future financial performance.**

Section 2

ANSWERS TO PRACTICE QUESTIONS

STATUTORY FINANCIAL STATEMENTS FOR A LIMITED COMPANY

1   ABC LTD

Journal entries for the additional data:

	Dr	Cr
	£000	£000
Inventory SFP	9,974	
Inventory SPL		9,974
Prepayment SFP 1024 × 3/12 = 256	256	
Administrative expenses SPL		256
Distribution costs SPL	132	
Accruals SFP 198 × 2/3 = 132		132
Interest SPL	1,120	
Interest payable SFP 28,000 × 8% × 6/12		1,120
Retained earnings	2,500	
Share capital		2,500
Taxation SPL	1,960	
Tax payable SFP		1,960

ABC Ltd

(a) **Statement of profit or loss for the year ended 31/10/X9**

	£000
Revenue (W1)	92,866
Cost of sales (W2)	(64,064)
Gross profit	28,802
Distribution costs (W3)	(5,032)
Administrative expenses (W4)	(6,632)
Profit from operations	17,138
Finance costs (W5)	(2,240)
Profit before tax	14,898
Tax	(1,960)
Profit for the period	12,938
Other comprehensive income for the year	0
Total comprehensive income for the year	12,938

Workings

(W1) Revenue

	£000
Sales	93,554
Less returns inwards	(688)
Total	92,866

(W2) COS

	£000
Opening inventories	8,932
Purchases	65,552
Less returns out	(446)
Less closing inventories	(9,974)
Total	64,064

(W3) Distribution costs

	£000
Distribution costs	4,900
Accrual	132
Total	5,032

(W4) Administrative expenses

	£000
Administrative expenses	6,888
Prepayment	(256)
Total	6,632

(W5) Finance costs

	£000
Finance costs	1,120
Accrual	1,120
Total	2,240

(b)   Statement of financial position as at 31/10/X9

	£000
ASSETS	
Non-current assets	
Property, plant and equipment (W1)	36,200
Current assets	
Inventories	9,974
Trade and other receivables (W2)	4,724
Cash and cash equivalents	19,308
	34,006
Total assets	70,206
EQUITY AND LIABILITIES	
Equity	
Share capital (18,000 + 2,500)	20,500
Retained earnings (W3)	15,508
Total equity	36,008

Non-current liabilities

Bank loans   28,000

Current liabilities

Trade and other payables (W4)   4,238

Tax payable   1,960

Total liabilities   34,198

Equity and liabilities   70,206

Workings

(W1) PPE

	£000
Property, plant and equipment cost	79,760
Accumulated depreciation	(43,560)
Total	36,200

(W2) Trade and other receivables

	£000
Trade and other receivables	4,468
Prepayment	256
Total	4,724

(W3) Retained earnings

	£000
Retained earnings	6,930
Profit from IS	12,938
Final dividend	(1,080)
Interim dividend	(780)
Bonus issue	(2,500)
Total	15,508

(W4) Trade and other payables

	£000
Trade and other payables	2,694
Accruals	292
Interest	1,120
Distribution costs	132
Total	4,238

(c)   **Statement of changes in equity**

	Share capital	Retained earnings	Total
Bal b/f	18,000	6,930	24,930
Bonus issue	2,500	(2,500)	0
Profit		12,938	12,938
Dividends		(1,080)	(1,860)
		(780)	
Bal c/f	20,500	15,508	36,008

2   WILLOW LTD

(a)   **Willow Ltd – Statement of profit or loss and other comprehensive income for the year ended 30 June 20X1**

	£000
Revenue	100,926
Cost of sales (W1)	(67,051)
	————
Gross profit	33,875
Distribution costs (W2)	(7,826)
Administrative expenses (W3)	(11,761)
	————
Profit from operations	14,288
Finance costs (W4)	(1,000)
	————
Profit before tax	13,288
Tax	(2,700)
	————
Profit for the period	10,588
Other comprehensive income for the year	
Gain on revaluation of the land (54,000 – 40,000) (W5)	14,000
	————
Total comprehensive income for the year	24,588
	————

Workings

(W1) COS

	£000
Opening inventories	7,280
Purchases	67,231
Less closing inventories	(9,420)
Depreciation P&M ((32,000 − 18,000) × 20% × 70%)	1,960
Total	67,051

(W2) Distribution costs

	£000
Distribution costs	8,326
Depreciation P&M ((32,000 − 18,000) × 20% × 20%)	560
Prepayment (2,120 × 6/12)	(1,060)
Total	7,826

(W3) Administrative expenses

	£000
Administrative expenses	7,741
Depreciation buildings ((120,000 − 40,000) × 4%)	3,200
Depreciation P&M ((32,000 − 18,000) × 20% × 10%)	280
Irrecoverable debt w/off	540
Total	11,761

(W4) Finance costs

	£000
Finance costs	0
Accrual (20,000 × 5%)	1,000
Total	1,000

(W5) Revaluation

	£000
Revalued amount	54,000
CA	40,000
Revaluation surplus	14,000

(b) **Willow Ltd – Statement of financial position as at 30 June 20X1**

Willow	£000
ASSETS	
Non-current assets	
Property, plant and equipment (W1)	119,500
Current assets	
Inventories	9,420
Trade and other receivables (W2)	20,800
Cash and cash equivalents	2,213
	32,433
Total assets	151,933
EQUITY AND LIABILITIES	
Equity	
Share capital	50,000
Share premium	25,000
Retained earnings (W3)	20,508
Revaluation surplus	24,000
Total equity	119,508
Non-current liabilities	
5% bank loan	20,000
	20,000
Current liabilities	
Trade and other payables (W4)	9,725
Tax liability	2,700
	12,425
Total liabilities	32,425
Equity and liabilities	151,933

Workings

(W1) PPE

	£000
Land and buildings cost	120,000
Revaluation	14,000
Accumulated depreciation	(22,500)
Depreciation charge	(3,200)
Plant and equipment cost	32,000
Accumulated depreciation	(18,000)
Depreciation charge	(2,800)
Total	119,500

(W2) Trade and other receivables

	£000
Trade and other receivables	20,280
Irrecoverable debt w/off	(540)
Prepayments (2,120 × 6/12)	1,060
Total	20,800

(W3) Retained earnings

	£000
Retained earnings	12,920
Profit P/L	10,588
Dividends	(3,000)
Total	20,508

(W4) Trade and other payables

	£000
Trade and other payables	8,725
Accruals (20,000 × 5%)	1,000
Total	9,725

3   CLERC LTD

(a)   **Clerc Ltd – Statement of profit or loss and other comprehensive income for the year ended 31 December 20X9**

	£000
Revenue	178,833
Cost of sales (W1)	(146,920)
Gross profit	31,913
Distribution costs	(7,009)
Administrative expenses (W2)	(14,820)
Profit from operations	10,084
Investment income	100
Finance costs (W3)	(2,000)
Profit before tax	8,184
Tax	(7,162)
Profit for the period	1,022
Other comprehensive income for the year	
Gain on revaluation of the land (150,000 – 110,000) (W4)	40,000
Total comprehensive income for the year	41,022

Workings

(W1) COS

	£000
Opening inventories	17,331
Purchases	130,562
Less closing inventories (19,871 – 500w/0ff)	(19,371)
Depreciation building ((210,000 – 110,000) × 10% × 40%)	4,000
Depreciation plant ((88,000 – 16,010) × 20%)	14,398
Total	146,920

(W2) Administrative expenses

	£000
Administrative expenses	7,100
Depreciation – buildings ((210,000 – 110,000) × 10% × 60%)	6,000
Irrecoverable debt w/off	1,720
Total	14,820

(W3) Finance costs

	£000
Finance costs	0
Accrual (40,000 × 5%)	2,000
Total	2,000

(W4) Revaluation of land

	£000
Revalued amount	150,000
CA	(110,000)
Revaluation surplus	40,000

(b) **Clerc Ltd – Statement of financial position as at 31 December 20X9**

	£000
ASSETS	
Non-current assets	
Property, plant and equipment (W1)	267,592
Current assets	
Inventories	19,371
Trade and other receivables (W2)	7,032
Cash and cash equivalents	6,993
	33,396
Total assets	300,988
EQUITY AND LIABILITIES	
Equity	
Share capital	100,000
Share premium	20,000
Retained earnings (W3)	24,915
Revaluation surplus (50,000 + 40,000 reval'n)	90,000
Total equity	234,915

Non-current liabilities

Bank loans	40,000
	40,000

Current liabilities

Trade and other payables (W4)	18,911
Tax liability	7,162
	26,073

Total liabilities	66,073

Equity and liabilities	300,988

Workings

(W1) PPE

	£000
Land and buildings cost	210,000
Revaluation	40,000
Accumulated depreciation	(30,000)
Depreciation charge	(10,000)
Plant and machinery cost	88,000
Accumulated depreciation	(16,010)
Depreciation charge	(14,398)
Total	267,592

(W2) Trade and other receivables

	£000
Trade and other receivables	8,752
Irrecoverable debt w/off	(1,720)
Total	7,032

(W3) Retained earnings

	£000
Retained earnings	23,893
Profit	1,022
Total	24,915

(W4) Trade and other payables

	£000
Trade and other payables	13,882
Accruals	3,029
Interest (40,000 × 5%)	2,000
Total	18,911

4   RCH LTD

(a)   **RCH Ltd – Statement of profit or loss and other comprehensive income for the year ended 31 March 20X1**

	£
Revenue	480,742
Cost of sales (W1)	(177,000)
Gross profit	303,742
Distribution costs (W2)	(32,239)
Administrative expenses (W3)	(44,459)
Profit from operations	227,044
Finance costs (W4)	(1,820)
Profit before tax	225,224
Tax	(33,740)
Profit for the period	191,484
Other comprehensive income for the year	
Gain on revaluation of the land (W5)	51,000
Total comprehensive income for the year	242,484

Workings

(W1) COS

	£000
Opening inventories	84,220
Purchases	153,444
Less closing inventories	(77,004)
Depreciation buildings	4,355
Deprecation plant and equipment	11,985
Total	177,000

(W2) Distribution costs

	£000
Distribution costs	23,587
Depreciation buildings	1,089
Depreciation plant	2,996
Accrual	4,567
Total	32,239

(W3) Administrative expenses

	£000
Administrative expenses	36,811
Irrecoverable debt w/off	840
Depreciation buildings	1,814
Depreciation plant	4,994
Total	44,459

(W4) Finance costs

	£000
Interest paid	910
Accrual	910
Total	1,820

(W5) Revaluation

	£000
Revalued amount	151,000
CA	100,000
Total	51,000

(b)   RCH Ltd – Statement of financial position as at 31 March 20X1

	£000
ASSETS	
Non-current assets	
Property, plant and equipment (W1)	319,785
Current assets	
Inventories	77,004
Trade and other receivables (W2)	11,336
Cash and cash equivalents	–
	88,340
Total assets	408,125
EQUITY AND LIABILITIES	
Equity	
Share capital	50,000
Retained earnings (W3)	202,001
Revaluation surplus	63,500
Total equity	315,501
Non-current liabilities	
Bank loans	26,000
	26,000
Current liabilities	
Trade and other payables (W4)	32,036
Overdraft	848
Tax liability	33,740
	66,624
Total liabilities	92,624
Equity and liabilities	408,125

Workings

(W1) PPE

	£000
Land and buildings at cost	281,450
Revaluation	51,000
Accumulated depreciation	(65,332)
Depreciation charge	(7,258)
Plant and equipment cost	94,400
Accumulated depreciation	(14,500)
Depreciation charge	(19,975)
Total	319,785

(W2) Trade and other receivables

	£000
Trade and other receivables	12,176
Irrecoverable debts w/off	(840)
Total	11,336

(W3) Retained earnings

	£000
Retained earnings	12,017
Profit (P/L)	191,484
Dividend	(1,500)
Total	202,001

(W4) Trade and other payables

	£000
Trade and other payables	25,342
Distribution accrual	4,567
Interest accrual	910
Accruals	1,217
Total	32,036

5 MAGNOLIA LTD

(a) Reconciliation of profit from operations to net cash from operating activities

	£000
Profit before tax	13,701
Adjustments for:	
Depreciation	6,700
Finance costs	1,052
Dividends received	(280)
Loss on disposal of property, plant and equipment	575
Decrease/(increase) in inventories (W1)	(2,367)
Decrease/(increase) in trade receivables (W1)	2,150
(Decrease)/increase in trade payables (W1)	(4,737)
	———
Cash generated by operations	16,794
Tax paid (W4)	(2,130)
Interest paid (W2)	(1,045)
	———
Net cash from operating activities	13,619
	———

(b) Magnolia Ltd – Statement of cash flows for year ended 31 March 20X1

	£000
Net cash from operating activities	13,619
Investing activities	
Dividends received	280
Proceeds on disposal of property, plant and equipment (W3)	725
Purchases of property, plant and equipment (W5)	(20,720)
	———
Net cash used in investing activities	(19,715)
Financing activities	
New bank loans raised (W6)	2,400
Proceeds of share issue (W7)	6,000
Dividends paid	(1,200)
	———
Net cash from financing activities	7,200
	———
Net increase in cash and cash equivalents	1,104
	———
Cash and cash equivalents at beginning of year	(432)
	———
Cash and cash equivalents at end of year	672
	———

(c) **Magnolia Ltd – Statement of changes in equity for the year ended 31 March 20X1**

	Share capital	Other reserves	Retained earnings	Total equity
Balance at 1 April 20X0	7,200	4,800	48,539	60,539
Changes in equity for 20X1				
Profit for the year			9,861	9,861
Dividends			(1,200)	(1,200)
Issue of share capital	3,600	2,400		6,000
Balance at 31 March 20X1	10,800	7,200	57,200	75,200

Workings

(W1) Changes in working capital

	£000 20X0	£000 20X1	Increase/ Decrease
Inventories	11,827	14,194	2,367 inc
Trade receivables	12,902	10,752	2,150 dec
Trade payables	10,644 – 78	5,914 – 85	4,737 dec

(W2) Interest paid

	£000
Accrual b/f	78
Statement of profit or loss charge	1,052
Accrual c/f	(85)
Total	1,045

(W3) Proceeds on disposal of PPE

	£000
CA	1,300
Loss on disposal	(575)
Proceeds	725

(W4) Tax paid

	£000
Accrual b/f	2,130
Statement of profit or loss charge	3,840
Accrual c/f	(3,840)
Total	2,130

(W5) Purchase of PPE

	£000
Balance b/f	50,216
Disposals @ CA (2,100 – 800)	(1,300)
Depreciation charge	(6,700)
Balance c/f	(62,936)
Purchase of PPE	20,720

(W6) Bank loans raised/redeemed

	£000 20X0	£000 20X1	Increase/ Decrease
Bank loans	1,200	3,600	2,400 inc

(W7) Share issue

	£000 20X0	£000 20X1	Increase/ Decrease
Share capital	7,200	10,800	3,600 inc
Share premium	4,800	7,200	2,400 inc
Total			6,000 inc

6 THORNGUMBALD LTD

(a) **Thorngumbald Ltd – Reconciliation of profit from operations to net cash from operating activities**

	£000
Profit before tax	13,470
Adjustments for:	
Depreciation	8,916
Finance costs	210
Dividends received	(240)
Gain on disposal of PPE (W2)	(896)
Decrease/(increase) in inventories (W1)	(1,972)
Decrease/(increase) in trade receivables (W1)	1,792
(Decrease)/increase in trade payables (W1)	(3,942)
Cash generated by operations	17,338
Tax paid	(1,774)
Interest paid	(210)
Net cash from operating activities	15,354

(b) **Thorngumbald Ltd – Statement of cash flows for year ended 31 March 20X9**

	£000
Net cash from operating activities	15,354
Investing activities	
Dividends received	240
Proceeds on disposal of PPE	1,984
Purchases of PPE (W3)	(23,104)
Net cash used in investing activities	(20,880)
Financing activities	
New bank loans raised (W4)	2,000
Proceeds of share issue (W5)	5,000
Dividends paid	(554)
Net cash from financing activities	6,446
Net increase in cash and cash equivalents	920
Cash and cash equivalents at beginning of year	(360)
Cash and cash equivalents at end of year	560

(c) **Thorngumbald Ltd – Statement of changes in equity for the year ended 31 March 20X9**

	Share capital	Other reserves	Retained earnings	Total equity
Balance at 1 April 20X8	6,000	4,000	41,284	51,284
Changes in equity for 20X9				
Profit for the year			7,702	7,702
Dividends			(554)	(554)
Share issue	3,000	2,000		5,000
Balance at 31 March 20X9	**9,000**	**6,000**	**48,432**	**63,432**

Workings

(W1) Changes in working capital

	£000 20X8	£000 20X9	Increase/ Decrease
Inventories	9,856	11,828	1,972 inc
Trade receivables	10,752	8,960	1,792 dec
Trade payables	8,870	4,928	3,942 dec

(W2) Proceeds on disposal of PPE

	£000
CA	1,088
Gain on disposal	896
Proceeds	1,984

(W3) Purchase of PPE

	£000
Balance b/f	42,680
Disposals @ CA	(1,088)
Depreciation charge	(8,916)
Balance c/f	(55,780)
Purchase of PPE	23,104

(W4) Bank loans raised/redeemed

	£000 20X8	£000 20X9	Increase/ Decrease
Bank loans	1,000	3,000	2,000 inc

(W5) Share issue

	£000 20X8	£000 20X9	Increase/ Decrease
Share capital	6,000	9,000	3,000 inc
Share premium	4,000	6,000	2,000 inc
Total			5,000 inc

7   DEAN LTD

(a)   **Reconciliation of profit from operations to net cash from operating activities**

	£000
Profit before tax	19,100
Adjustments for:	
Finance costs	1200
Dividends received	(2000)
Interest received	(300)
Depreciation	6,235
Gain on disposal of property, plant and equipment (W2)	(1,200)
Decrease/(increase) in inventories (W1)	1,800
Decrease/(increase) in trade receivables (W1)	(1,960)
(Decrease)/increase in trade payables (W1)	(5,005)
	———
Cash generated by operations	17,870
Tax paid	(1,820)
Interest paid	(1,200)
	———
Net cash from operating activities	14,850
	———

(b)   **Dean Ltd – Statement of cash flows for year ended 31 March 20X9**

	£000
Net cash from operating activities	14,850
Investing activities	
Dividends received	2,000
Interest received	300
Proceeds on disposal of property, plant and equipment	13,100
Purchases of property, plant and equipment (W3)	(24,755)
	———
Net cash used in investing activities	(9,355)
Financing activities	
Redemption of bank loan (W4)	(10,000)
Proceeds of share issue (W5)	8,000
Dividends paid (W6)	(5,000)
	———
Net cash from financing activities	(7,000)
Net increase/(decrease) in cash and cash equivalents	(1,505)
Cash and cash equivalents at beginning of year	935
	———
Cash and cash equivalents at end of year	(570)
	———

(c)   Dean Ltd – Statement of changes in equity for the year ended 31 March 20X9

	Share capital	Share premium	Revaln surplus	Retained earnings	Total equity
Balance at 1 April 20X8	25,000	2,000	0	35,550	62,550
Changes in equity for 20X9					
Profit for the year				15,280	15,280
Revaluation in year			5,000		5,000
Dividends				(5,000)	(5,000)
Issue of share capital	5,000	3,000			8,000
Balance at 31 March 20X9	30,000	5,000	5,000	45,830	85,830

Workings

(W1) Changes in working capital

	£000 20X8	£000 20X9	Increase/ Decrease
Inventories	12,100	10,300	1,800 dec
Trade receivables	14,320	16,280	1,960 inc
Trade payables	14,505	9,500	5,005 dec

(W2) Gain/loss on disposal of PPE

	£000
Proceeds	13,100
Carrying amount	(11,900)
Gain on disposal	1,200

(W3) Purchase of PPE

	£000
Balance b/f	68,200
Disposals @ CA	(11,900)
Depreciation charge	(6,235)
Revaluation	5,000
Balance c/f	(79,820)
Purchase of PPE	24,755

(W4) Bank loans raised/redeemed

	£000 20X8	£000 20X9	Increase/ Decrease
Bank loans	15,000	5,000	10,000 dec

(W5) Share issue

	£000 **20X8**	£000 **20X9**	Increase/ **Decrease**
Share capital	25,000	30,000	5,000
Share premium	2,000	5,000	3,000
Total			8,000 inc

(W6) Dividends paid

	£000
20X8 retained earnings	35,550
Profit	15,280
20X9 retained earnings	(45,830)
Dividend paid	5,000

8 ROSSINGTON LTD

(a) Reconciliation of profit from operations to net cash from operating activities

	£000
Profit before tax	142
Adjustments for:	
Depreciation	255
Finance costs	40
Dividends received	(20)
Gain on disposal of property, plant and equipment	(3)
Decrease/(increase) in inventories	30
Decrease/(increase) in trade receivables	85
(Decrease)/increase in trade payables	(205)
Cash generated by operations	324
Tax paid	(47)
Interest paid	(40)
Net cash from operating activities	237

(b)   Rossington Ltd – Statement of cash flows for year ended 31 March 20X1

	£000
Net cash from operating activities	237
Investing activities	
Dividends received	20
Proceeds on disposal of property, plant and equipment	15
Purchases of property, plant and equipment	(767)
Net cash used in investing activities	(732)
Financing activities	
New bank loans raised	275
Proceeds of share issue	265
Dividends paid	(65)
Net cash from financing activities	475
Net increase/(decrease) in cash and cash equivalents	(20)
Cash and cash equivalents at beginning of year (35 – 40)	(5)
Cash and cash equivalents at end of year (0 – 25)	(25)

(c)   Rossington Ltd – Statement of changes in equity for the year ended 31 March 20X1

	Share capital £000	Other reserves £000	Retained earnings £000	Total equity £000
Balance at 1 April 20X0	300	85	990	1,375
Changes in equity for 20X1				
Profit for the year			85	85
Dividends			(65)	(65)
Issue of share capital	200	65		265
Balance at 31 March 20X1	500	150	1,010	1,660

Workings

(W1) Changes in working capital

	£000 20X0	£000 20X1	Increase/ Decrease
Inventories	510	480	30 dec
Trade receivables	435	350	85 dec
Trade payables	555	350	205 dec

(W2) Gain/loss on disposal of PPE

	£000
Proceeds	15
CA	(12)
Gain on disposal	3

(W3) Purchase of PPE

	£000
Balance b/f	1,065
Disposals @ CA	(12)
Depreciation charge	(255)
Balance c/f	(1,565)
Purchase of PPE	767

(W4) Bank loans raised/redeemed

	£000 20X0	£000 20X1	Increase/ Decrease
Bank loans	25	300	275 inc

(W5) Share issue

	£000 20X0	£000 20X1	Increase/ Decrease
Share capital	300	500	200
Share premium	150	85	65
Total			265

(W6) Dividends paid

	£000
20X8 retained earnings	990
Profit	85
20X9 retained earnings	(1,010)
Dividend paid	65

9 RAINFORD LTD

(a) **Rainford Ltd – Reconciliation of profit from operations to net cash from operating activities**

	£000
Profit before tax	142
Adjustments for:	
Dividends received and gain on investments	(20)
Finance costs	40
Depreciation	200
Gain on disposal of property, plant and equipment (per SPL)	(80)
Decrease/(increase) in inventories (W1)	30
Decrease/(increase) in trade receivables (W1)	110
(Decrease)/increase in trade payables (W1)	(202)
	——
Cash generated by operations	220
Tax paid (opening liability paid)(W4)	(50)
Interest paid (W2)	(40)
	——
Net cash from operating activities	130
	——

(b) **Rainford Ltd – Statement of cash flows for year ended 30 September 20X3**

	£000
Net cash from operating activities	130
Investing activities	
Dividends received (per SPL)	20
Proceeds on disposal of property, plant and equipment (W3)	100
Purchases of property, plant and equipment (W5)	(560)
Purchases of investments (£285 – £125)	(160)
	——
Net cash used in investing activities	(600)
Financing activities	
New bank loans raised (W6)	275
Proceeds of share issue (W7)	265
Dividends paid (W8)	(65)
	——
Net cash from financing activities	475
Net increase/(decrease) in cash and cash equivalents (W9)	5
Net cash and cash equivalents at beginning of year (W9)	50
	——
Net cash and cash equivalents at end of year (W9)	55
	——

Workings

(W1) Changes in working capital

	£000 20X3	£000 20X2	Increase/ Decrease
Inventories	480	510	30 dec
Trade receivables	270	380	110 dec
Trade payables	353	555	202 dec

(W2) Interest paid

	£000
Accrual b/f	Nil
Profit or loss charge	40
Accrual c/f	Nil
Cash paid	40

(W3) Proceeds on disposal of PPE

	£000
CA	20
Gain on disposal (per SPL)	80
Proceeds	100

(W4) Tax paid

	£000
Accrual b/f	50
Profit or loss charge	57
Accrual c/f	(57)
Cash paid	50

(W5) Purchase of PPE

	£000
Balance b/f	940
Disposals @ CA	(20)
Depreciation charge	(200)
Balance c/f	(1,280)
Cash paid to purchase PPE	560

(W6) Bank loans raised/redeemed

	£000 20X3	£000 20X2	Increase/ Decrease
Bank loans	300	25	275 inc

(W7) Share issue

	£000 20X3	£000 20X2	Increase/ Decrease
Share capital	500	300	200 inc
Share premium	150	85	65 inc
Total			265 inc

(W8) Retained earnings

	£000
Balance b/f	990
Profit for the year (per SPL)	85
Dividend for the year	(65)
Balance c/f	(1,010)

(W9) Cash and equivalents

	£000 20X3	£000 20X2	Increase/ Decrease
Cash and equivalents	80	90	10 dec
Overdraft	(25)	(40)	15 inc
Net balance	55	50	5 inc

(c)   Rainford Ltd – Statement of changes in equity for the year ended 30 September 20X3

	Share capital	Share premium	Retained earnings	Total equity
	£000	£000	£000	£000
Balance at 1 October 20X2	300	85	990	1,375
Changes in equity for the year				
Profit for the year			85	85
Dividends paid in the year			(65)	(65)
Issue of share capital	200	65		265
	———	———	———	———
Balance at 30 September 20X3	500	150	1,010	1,660
	———	———	———	———

REGULATORY AND CONCEPTUAL FRAMEWORKS AND DIFFERENT TYPES OF ORGANISATIONS

10 RECOGNITION

(a) **(i)** 'An asset is a **present economic resource** controlled by an entity as a result of a **past event**' (para 4.3)

(ii) 'A liability is a **present obligation** of the entity to transfer an **economic resource** as a result of a **past event'** (para 4.26)

(iii) 'Equity is the residual interest in the assets of the entity after deducting all its liabilities.' (para 4.63)

(b) Recognition is the process of incorporating in the statements an item that meets the definition of an element and satisfies the following criteria for recognition:

- It provides relevant information regarding the particular element.

- It provides a faithful representation of the particular element.

11 OBJECTIVES

(a) The objective of financial statements according to the framework is:

'to provide information about an entity's assets, liabilities, equity, income and expenses that is useful to financial statements users in assessing the prospects of future net cash inflows to the entity and in assessing management's stewardship of the entity's resources'.

(b) The external users and their need for information in financial statements would include:

Investors:	To decide whether to purchase new shares in the company, retain their current shares or sell them.
Potential investors:	To determine whether to invest in shares in the company.
Lenders:	Does the company have the ability to pay back their loans and interest payments or whether to lend them money.
Suppliers:	Does the company have the ability to pay what is due to them.
Customers:	Will the company be trading in the foreseeable future so that their product/service can still be supplied to them.
Government:	Statistical purposes and taxation.
Public:	Interested in the contribution of entities to the local economy.

12   FUNDAMENTAL CHARACTERISTICS

(a)   The fundamental qualitative characteristics are relevance and faithful representation.

(b)   Expenses are defined as 'decreases in economic benefits during the accounting period in the form of outflows or depletions of assets or incurrences of liabilities that result in decreases in equity, other than those relating to distributions to equity participants.' [F4.49]

13   CONCEPTUAL FRAMEWORK

(a)   The two fundamental characteristics of useful financial information are as follows:

1   **Relevance**

Information is relevant if it is capable of **influencing the decisions of users**.

The Framework document recognises that different users have different information requirements to make their decisions. For example, shareholders (primary users) will want information to review the risks and returns associated with their investment to decide whether to buy, retain or sell shares in a company.

2   **Faithful representation**

Faithful representation means that information must be **complete, neutral and free from error**. In effect, financial statements produced should show a true and fair view.

This means that information can be relied upon by users of financial information as part of their decision-making procedures. If information was incomplete, or biased or contained significant errors, it could not be relied upon for decision-making purposes. If such information was relied upon for decision-making purposes, it is likely the users of that information would make inappropriate or wrong decisions.

(b)   The definition of a liability and an expense are as follows:

1   **Liability**

A liability is a present obligation of the entity to transfer an economic resource as a result of a past event. An example of a liability is an amount due to a supplier for goods or services already received by a business. Liabilities are classified on the statement of financial position as either non-current liabilities or current liabilities, depending upon when they fall due for payment. (**Note:** Any example would earn marks.)

2   **Expense**

An expense represents a **decrease** or using up **of economic benefits** during an accounting period. Examples of this include the wages costs of employees. (**Note:** Any example would earn marks.)

14 JACOB

(a)   Companies registered in the UK would need to follow the provisions of the Companies Act 2006, which has guidance and rules on the format of financial statements, how to value items in the financial statements and the fundamental accounting principles. The company would also need to follow a set of accounting standards, for example the International Financial Reporting Standards (IFRS).

(b)   Accounting standards help to make sure that every company is treating similar transactions in the same way and including the same level of information in their financial statements. This helps to reduce the degree of subjectivity within a set of financial statements and therefore makes them more comparable, from one year to the next and from one company to another.

15 QUALITATIVE CHARACTERISTICS

(iii) Reliability is not one of the 'enhancing' characteristics.

16 PUBLIC AND PRIVATE LIMITED COMPANIES

	True	False
A private limited company is required to have a minimum of two members		✓
Both private and public limited companies are required to file their accounts on an annual basis	✓	
Private limited companies may be exempt from an annual audit, but public companies cannot be exempt	✓	
Public limited companies need to have at least £40,000 of issued share capital		✓

A public limited company is required to have a minimum of two members.

Public limited companies need to have at least £50,000 of issued share capital.

17 SOLE TRADER VS LIMITED COMPANIES

B – All of the statements are true apart from the first statement. The statement of profit or loss for a sole trader should not show taxation as a business expense.

18 AL

The owners of a limited company are the shareholders (investors). They have limited liability for debts incurred by the business, which means they are only accountable for the value of the shares they own but have not yet paid for. If all shares are paid up, the shareholder's liability for company debts is limited to that money invested. A sole trader has unlimited liability which means that they are personally liable for the business' debts.

Tax does not appear in a sole trader's statement of profit or loss. However, limited companies are taxed on their profits, and this is charged to the statement of profit or loss as an expense. It is recorded as a liability in the statement of financial position until it is paid.

Sole traders both own and manage their business, so they have full control over business decisions. Limited companies are managed by the directors on behalf of the shareholders.

Sole traders are not legally required to produce annual accounts or file accounts for inspection. However, a record of business expenses and personal income are required for tax returns. A limited company must prepare annual accounts (also known as 'statutory accounts') at the end of the financial year. The annual accounts should be accompanied by disclosure notes. These are filed with HMRC as part of its tax return and also sent to all shareholders and Companies House. Company accounts must be prepared in line with accounting standards.

A sole trader has the flexibility to take drawings from the business for personal expenses. Shareholders cannot make withdrawals from the business in the way that a sole trader is able to do.

Instead, they receive a return on their investment in the company referred to as a dividend which is paid from accumulated profits. Dividends for limited companies are the equivalent of drawings for a sole trader.

INTERNATIONAL FINANCIAL REPORTING STANDARDS (WRITTEN QUESTIONS)

19   OAK PLC

(a)   **Why is land not depreciated?**

Depreciation is the application of the accruals concept and matching the cost of purchasing an asset to the benefits received over the assets useful economic life. Buildings have a finite useful life. If they will provide benefits for fifty years, then this should be matched with the expense over fifty years. Land has an indefinite life and therefore does not need to be depreciated.

(b)   **When properties are revalued why is there a difference in the accounting treatment for a revaluation surplus and a revaluation decrease?**

With an upwards revaluation the company makes a surplus (gain) that is not yet realised and therefore cannot be part of retained earnings, so a separate revaluation surplus is created. With a downwards revaluation, the decrease is first set against any revaluation surplus for that asset, with any further decreases recognised immediately in the statement of profit or loss. This is as an application of the prudence concept whereby losses are recognised sooner than gains which are only recognised when they are realised.

(c)   **Why does IAS 16 *Property, Plant and Equipment* permit a transfer within equity for the annual 'excess depreciation' charge arising as a result of revaluation of a building?**

This is recognition that part of the revaluation surplus relating to a revalued building has become a realised gain. Therefore, companies are permitted to make an annual transfer within the statement of changes in equity from revaluation surplus to retained earnings for the increase in the depreciation charge as a result of revaluing the building.

20 VICTORIA PLC

(a) An intangible asset according to IAS 38 *Intangible Assets* is

'an identifiable non-monetary asset without physical substance'.

(b) Development costs can be recognised as an asset in the statement of financial position when the following criteria have been fulfilled:

- the availability of adequate technical, financial and other resources to complete the development and to use or sell the intangible asset

- the technical feasibility of completing the intangible asset so that it will be available for use or sale

- its intention to complete the intangible asset and use or sell it

- its ability to use or sell the intangible asset

- how the intangible asset will generate future economic benefits

- its ability to measure reliably the expenditure attributable to the intangible asset during its development.

21 POPPY PLC

(a) At the commencement of a lease, the lessee should recognise a lease liability and a right-of-use asset in the statement of financial position.

The lease liability is initially measured at the present value of the lease payments that have not yet been paid.

The right of use asset is initially recognised at cost which comprises:

- The amount of the initial measurement of the lease liability (as above)

- Lease payments made at or before the commencement date

- Any initial direct costs

- The estimated costs of removing or dismantling the underlying asset as per the conditions of the lease.

(b) A right-of-use asset is measured using the cost model. This means that the asset is measured at its initial cost less accumulated depreciation and impairment losses.

Depreciation is calculated as follows:

- If ownership of the asset transfers to the lessee at the end of the lease term then depreciation should be charged over the asset's useful life,

- Otherwise, depreciation is charged over the shorter of the useful life and the lease term.

22   TODDY PLC

(a)   A provision is recognised when:

- There is an obligation as a result of a past event.

- It is probable that there will be an outflow of resources to settle the obligation.

- A reliable estimate can be made of the amount of the obligation.

(b)   A provision should not be recognised because it is only possible that Toddy plc will lose the case and have to pay money to the employee. To recognise a provision, there must be a **probable** outflow.

Toddy plc should disclose this contingent liability in the notes to their financial statements.

(c)   IAS 37 **does not permit** a provision to be made in respect of future operating losses. Such losses are not regarded as an obligation – **they are regarded as being avoidable**. If Toddy plc terminated those activities immediately during 20X1, the losses in 20X2 would not be incurred.

23   ORMSKIRK LTD

Briefing Notes for the Directors of Ormskirk Ltd

IAS 38 *Intangible Assets* – specific reference to brands

(a)   An intangible asset is an **identifiable non-monetary asset without physical substance**. This definition distinguishes an intangible asset from tangible assets (which have physical substance) and financial assets such as investments.

IAS 38 makes an important distinction between purchased and non-purchased (internally generated) brands. **Only purchased brands** can be accounted for as it is **not possible to reliably determine the cost of an internally generated brand**.

IAS 38 requires that intangible assets are recognised and accounted for if they meet the definition, their cost can be reliably measured and if it is probable that they will generate future economic benefits for the business.

If such assets have a finite useful life, they should be amortised over their expected useful life to the business. The annual amortisation charge is an expense charged to profit or loss. This is a similar accounting treatment to accounting for property, plant and equipment which is depreciated over its estimated useful life to the business.

Based upon the available information, the brand would be recognised as an intangible non-current asset at a cost of £100,000. It would then be subject to an annual amortisation charge of (£100,000/5 years) £20,000.

(b)   If the directors believe that an intangible asset has an indefinite life, then it **should not be amortised**. Instead, it would be subject to an **annual impairment review**. For example, using the information from the question, an intangible non-current asset of £100,000 would be recognised. Each year, there should be a review to **consider whether the recoverable amount has fallen below the carrying amount** of £100,000. If it has (e.g. damage to the brand) then the carrying amount would be reduced and the **loss charged to profit or loss**.

INTERNATIONAL FINANCIAL REPORTING STANDARDS (MULTIPLE CHOICE QUESTIONS)

24 FORMBY LTD AND OTHERS

Statement: Development expenditure must be written off as an expense to profit or loss as it is incurred.

(a) **Is this statement true or false?** **False**

Statement: Research expenditure must be written off as an expense to profit or loss as it is incurred.

(b) **Is this statement true or false?** **True**

(c) **What is the closing inventory valuation of Melling Ltd as at 30 June 20X5?**

Answer A £7,600

Product	Quantity	Lower of Cost or NRV £	Total value £
A	100	20	2,000
B	200	13	2,600
C	300	10	3,000
			7,600

(d) **(i)** **Does the claim received by the Birkdale Ltd represent an adjusting or non-adjusting event in accordance with IAS 10 *Events after the Reporting Period*?**

Yes – receipt of the claim is an adjusting event as it provides additional information of what the situation was at the reporting date.

(ii) **Based upon the available information, should Birkdale Ltd include a provision in the financial statements for the claim of £10,000 in accordance with IAS 37 *Provisions, Contingent Assets and Contingent Liabilities*?**

Yes – at the reporting date, it is probable that there will be an outflow of economic benefits as a result of a past transaction or event. The past transaction or event is the employee suffering injury as a result of using faulty machinery. There is a reliable estimate of the amount of the claim. The company should recognise a provision in the financial statements for the year ended 30 April 20X8 for £10,000.

(e) **(i)** **What is the amount of the operating activities cash flow that will be included in Kirkby Ltd's statement of cash flows for the year ended 30 November 20X4 in respect of taxation?**

This will be the cash flow that occurred in the year – a cash outflow of £25,100 paid during the year ended 30 November 20X4.

(ii) **What is the tax charge that will be included in Kirkby Ltd's statement of profit or loss for the year ended 30 November 20X4?**

This will be the estimated tax charge on profits for the year ended 30 November 20X4 of £26,500 plus the under-provision in respect of the tax due for the year ended 30 November 20X3 of £400 (£24,700 estimated and £25,100 actually paid). This gives a total = tax charge in the statement of profit or loss for the year ended 30 November 20X4 of £26,900.

(f) **£89**

The discount should be allocated to each part of the bundled sale. Applying the discount across each part gives revenue as follows:

Goods   £50   (£75 × £100/£150)

Installation   £17   (£25 × £100/£150)

Service   £33   (£50 × £100/£150)

The revenue in relation to the goods and installation should be recognised on 1 May 20X1. As 8 months of the service has been performed (from 1 May to 31 December 20X1), then £22 should be recognised (£33 × $^8/_{12}$).

This gives a total revenue for the year of 50 + 17 + 22 = £89.

IAS 2 INVENTORIES

25 **CHESTNUT PLC**

The answer is B.

The double entry for closing inventory is:

Dr Inventory

Cr Cost of sales

Therefore, cost of sales will be too large and gross and net profit will be under-stated.

26 **FIFO**

The answer is C.

There were 260 units from the opening inventory and purchases in the period, 170 units were sold which leaves 90 units, these will be the last units purchased so 40 units @ £18 and 50 units @ £14.

27 WILKIE LTD

The answer is D.

IAS 2 permits use of the FIFO and weighted average cost methods of valuing inventory but not LIFO. Inventory should be measured at the lower of cost and net realisable value. Inventories are written down to net realisable value on an item by item basis, or similar items may be grouped together and a comparison made between the total cost of each group of items and their net realisable value.

Given the above, the valuations of the three distinct types of inventory will therefore be:

Inventory

	£
Boat	47,600
Truck	16,800
Plane	25,800
	90,200

28 SALT AND PEPPER LTD

The answer is C.

Inventory is valued at the lower of cost and NRV. LIFO is not an acceptable way to determine cost.

Therefore inventory = 9,800 + 23,055 + 28,027 + 5,100 = £65,982.

IAS 7 STATEMENT OF CASH FLOWS

29 CASH FLOW

False

Although an increase in receivables will have a negative impact on cash flow overall – it will be in respect of 'Cash flows from operating activities' not 'Cash flows from financing activities'.

30 INDIRECT METHOD

False

Depreciation is a non-cash expense that should be added back to profit from operations.

31 DIRECT AND INDIRECT METHOD

False

'Cash generated from operations' is a factual figure. Therefore, the answer will be the same under both the direct and indirect methods.

IAS 10 EVENTS AFTER THE REPORTING PERIOD

32 IAS 10

The answer D.

(i), (ii) and (iii) are given in IAS 10 as an example of non-adjusting events.

(iv) is given in IAS 10 as an example of an adjusting event.

33 COLWYN LTD

The answer is C.

34 EL GUARDO

The answer is B.

35 FIRE

False

The event (fire) took place after the year end and is given in IAS 10 (para 22) as an example of a non-adjusting event.

36 EVENTS

The answer is D.

IAS 16 PROPERTY, PLANT AND EQUIPMENT

37 LARCH PLC

The answer is C.

Per IAS 16 any costs incurred in bringing the asset into its working condition, this would include everything except the training costs.

38 REVALUATION

A revaluation surplus will be recognised as a gain in the statement of other comprehensive income.

The answer is false.

39 ELLIOTT LTD

The answer is A.

IAS 17 LEASES

40 ASH PLC

The answer is D.

In accordance with IFRS 16 the right-of-use asset should be recognised at the amount of the initial measurement of the lease liability + lease payments made at or before the commencement date + any initial direct costs + estimated costs of removing or dismantling the asset.

£10,000 + £8,500 = £18,500

41 BECKI LTD

The answer is B.

The statement is false as where the ownership of an asset does not transfer to the lessee at the end of the lease then the asset should be depreciated over the shorter of the useful life and the lease term. In this case this would be 16 years.

42 AXEL LTD

The answer is C.

IFRS 16 permits simplified treatment of assets with a lease of 12 months or less. The simplified treatment allows the lease payments to be charged as an expense over the lease period, applying the accruals concept.

Annual lease rental expense = £500 + £1,000 + £1,000 = £2,500

Expense to 31 December 20X8 = £2,500 × 9/12 = £1,875

IAS 36 IMPAIRMENT OF ASSETS

43 FRANK LTD

The answer is C.

According to IAS 36, an asset is impaired when its carrying amount exceeds its recoverable amount, where the recoverable amount of an asset is the higher of its fair value less costs to sell and its value in use. On this basis, assets I and III are impaired.

44 BOVEY LTD

The answer is A.

45 LEMON LTD

The answer is C.

46 IMPAIRMENT

The answer is false.

An asset is impaired if its carrying amount is higher than its recoverable amount.

47   ANNUAL TESTING

The answer is false.

Intangible assets with an indefinite life and goodwill are tested for impairment annually. For other assets, the company must simply look out for indicators of impairment.

IAS 37 PROVISIONS, CONTINGENT LIABILITIES AND ASSETS

48   OBLIGATIONS

The answer is A.

This is the definition of a provision.

49   TELVIN LTD

The answer is C.

In accordance with IAS 37 *Provisions, Contingent Liabilities and Contingent Assets*, the claim succeeding is only possible so should be disclosed as a contingent liability but the costs will be incurred regardless so they need to be provided for.

50   KENYA LTD

The answer is B.

In accordance with IAS 37 this potential outflow is classed as a provision and should therefore be recognised in the financial statements. As the inflow of benefits is probable, it should be disclosed in the notes to the accounts.

51   CASEY LTD

The answer is C.

A provision will only be recognised where it is 'probable' that the outflow will occur and can be measured reliably.

IAS 38 INTANGIBLE ASSETS

52   GOODREP LTD

The answer is false.

This is an internally generated intangible asset. It should not be recognised because the cost to produce it cannot be accurately determined.

53   RESEARCH AND DEVELOPMENT

The answer is D.

In accordance with IAS 38 *Intangible Assets*, research costs must be written off as incurred, development costs should be capitalised if they meet certain criteria.

IFRS 15 REVENUE FROM CONTRACTS WITH CUSTOMERS

54   NOTEBY LTD

The answer is C.

IFRS 15 Revenue from Contracts with Customers requires that revenue should be recognised only when performance obligations have been satisfied. The performance obligation for both sales is to transfer a good to the customer. The performance obligation is satisfied at the point in time when control of the goods passes to the customer. This often occurs on delivery.

Note by has complied with the obligation to deliver the machine on 28 August 20X7 and transfers control to Pitt on that date. Revenue can therefore be recognised on this transaction.

Similarly, Damon collected the food mixers on 26 August 20X7 and assumed control on this date. This means that revenue can be recognised. A receivable should be recognised for any amounts due but not yet received on both transactions.

CONSOLIDATED FINANCIAL STATEMENTS

55   BRYSON PLC

Bryson – Consolidated statement of financial position as at 31 March 20X1

	£000
ASSETS	
Goodwill (W1)	1,729
Non-current assets (11,280 + 3,670 + 450)	15,400
Current assets (W4)	10,290
Total assets	27,419
EQUITY AND LIABILITIES	
Equity	
Share capital	7,200
Retained earnings (W3)	12,394
Non-controlling interest (W2)	1,635
Total equity	21,229
Non-current liabilities (1,440 + 1,180)	2,620
Current liabilities (W5)	3,570
Total liabilities	6,190
Total equity and liabilities	27,419

Workings

(W1) Calculate goodwill

Goodwill	£000
Consideration	6,720
Net assets of Stoppard Ltd at acquisition	
(4,800 + 672 + 450)	(5,922)
Non-controlling interest at acquisition (25% × 5,922)	1,481
	———
Goodwill at acquisition	2,279
Less impairment	(550)
	———
Goodwill in SFP	1,729

(W2) Calculate NCI

Non-controlling Interest	£000
Share capital attributable to NCI (25% × 4,800)	1,200
Retained earnings attributable to NCI (25% × 1,290)	322
Fair value adjustment attributable to NCI (25% × 450)	113
Total	1,635

(W3) Calculate retained earnings

Retained earnings	£000
Bryson plc	12,480
Stoppard post acq reserves (75% × (1,290 − 672))	464
Goodwill impairment	(550)
Total	12,394

(W4) Current assets

	£000
Bryson plc	5,760
Stoppard Ltd	5,010
Intercompany balance	(480)
Total	10,290

(W5) Current liabilities

	£000
Bryson plc	2,640
Stoppard Ltd	1,410
Intercompany balance	(480)
Total	3,570

56   SUGAR PLC

Sugar plc – Consolidated statement of profit or loss for the year ended 31 March 20X1

	£000
Revenue (W1)	142,164
Cost of sales (W2)	(76,060)
Gross profit	66,104
Distribution costs and administrative expenses (6,000 + 3,800)	(9,800)
Profit before tax	56,304

Workings

(W1) Revenue

	£000
Sugar plc	97,900
Brady Ltd	44,600
Intercompany transaction	(336)
Total	142,164

(W2) COS

	£000
Sugar plc	58,800
Brady Ltd	17,500
Intercompany transaction	(336)
Provision for unrealised profits (W3)	96
Total	76,060

(W3) Provision for unrealised profits

	£000
Selling price	336
Cost of goods	(240)
Unrealised profit	96

Note: Dividends from Brady Ltd of £4,000,000 must be excluded from the consolidated statement of profit or loss.

57 SPENCER PLC

Spencer plc – Consolidated statement of financial position as at 31 March 20X1

	£000
ASSETS	
Goodwill (W1)	720
Non-current assets (12,576 + 7,490)	20,066
Current assets (W4)	6,828
Total assets	27,614
EQUITY AND LIABILITIES	
Equity	
Share capital	5,000
Retained earnings (W3)	14,234
Non-controlling interest (W2)	2,748
Total equity	21,982
Non-current liabilities (2,880 + 1,200)	4,080
Current liabilities (W5)	1,552
Total liabilities	5,632
Total equity and liabilities	27,614

Workings

Group share

Spencer plc holding in Marks Ltd (1,300,000/2,000,000) × 100 = 65%

NCI = 35% (100% – 65%)

(W1) Calculate goodwill

Goodwill	£000
Consideration	5,400
Net assets of Marks Ltd at acquisition	
(2,000 + 5,200)	(7,200)
Non-controlling interest at acquisition (35% × 7,200)	2,520
Goodwill in SFP	720

(W2) Calculate NCI

Non-controlling Interest	£000
Share capital attributable to NCI (35% × 2,000)	700
Retained earnings attributable to NCI (35% × 5,850)	2,048
Total	2,748

(W3) Calculate retained earnings

Retained earnings	£000
Spencer plc	13,840
Marks Ltd post acq reserves (65% × (5,850 – 5,200))	422
Unrealised profit (W6)	(28)
Total	14,234

(W4) Current assets

	£000
Spencer plc	5,136
Marks Ltd	2,140
Intercompany transaction	(420)
Unrealised profit (W6)	(28)
Total	6,828

(W5) Current liabilities

	£000
Spencer plc	1,392
Marks Ltd	580
Intercompany transaction	(420)
Total	1,552

(W6) Unrealised profit

	£000	%
Sale price	420	100
Cost (420 × 80%)	(336)	(80)
Gross profit (% on sales)	84	20

One third of the goods remain in inventory so the unrealised profit adjustments is £28,000 (£84,000 × 1/3).

58   MITCHELL PLC

(a)   Mitchell plc – Consolidated statement of profit or loss for the year ended 31 March 20X1

	£000
Revenue (W1)	108,440
Cost of sales (W2)	(59,830)
Gross profit	48,610
Distribution costs (7,620 + 1,280)	(8,900)
Administrative expenses (8,430 + 950)	(9,380)
Profit from operating activities	30,330
Investment income (8,000 – (10,000 × 65%)	1,500
Profit before tax	31,830
Taxation (7,500 + 3,080)	(10,580)
Profit after tax	21,250

(b)   **Profit for the year attributable to:**

Non-controlling interest is £7,920 × 35% = £2,772

Equity holders of the parent is £21,250 – £2,772 = £18,478 (bal fig)

Workings

(W1) Revenue

	£000
Mitchell plc	86,720
Camper Ltd	22,920
Intercompany transaction	(1,200)
Total	108,440

(W2) COS

	£000
Mitchell plc	51,340
Camper Ltd	9,690
Intercompany transaction	(1,200)
Total	59,830

59   TIPPERS PLC

Tippers plc – Consolidated statement of financial position as at 31 March 20X1

	£000
ASSETS	
Goodwill (W1)	635
Non-current assets (3,800 + 2,530 + 400)	6,730
Current assets (W4)	5,490
Total assets	12,855
EQUITY AND LIABILITIES	
Equity	
Share capital	3,000
Retained earnings (W3)	5,519
Non-controlling interest (W2)	636
Total equity	9,155
Non-current liabilities (750 + 1,980)	2,730
Current liabilities (W5)	970
Total liabilities	3,700
Total equity and liabilities	12,855

Workings

(W1) Calculate goodwill

Goodwill	£000
Consideration	1,800
Net assets of Holmes Ltd at acquisition	
1,000 + 140 + (1,200 – 800)	(1,540)
Non-controlling interest at acquisition (30% × 1,540)	462
Goodwill at acquisition	722
Impairment 12%	(87)
Goodwill in SFP	635

(W2) Calculate NCI

Non-controlling Interest	£000
Share capital attributable to NCI (30% × 1,000)	300
Retained earnings attributable to NCI (30% × 720)	216
Fair value adjustment (30% × 400)	120
Total	636

(W3) Retained earnings

	£000
Tippers plc	5,200
Holmes Ltd post acq reserves (70% × (720 – 140))	406
Goodwill impairment	(87)
Total	5,519

(W4) Current assets

	£000
Tippers plc	4,000
Holmes Ltd	1,690
Intercompany transaction	(200)
Total	5,490

(W5) Current liabilities

	£000
Tippers plc	650
Holmes Ltd	520
Intercompany transaction	(200)
Total	970

60   LUCY PLC

Lucy plc – Consolidated statement of profit or loss for the year ended 31 March 20X1

	£
Revenue (W1)	1,426,590
Cost of sales (W2)	(1,119,880)
Gross profit	306,710
Other income – dividend from Colin Ltd	–
Distribution costs and administrative expenses (24,320 + 15,640)	(39,960)
Profit before tax	266,750
Attributable to:	
Equity holders of Lucy plc (bal fig)	253,515
Non-controlling interest (132,350 × 10%)	13,235
	266,750

Workings

(W1) Revenue

	£
Lucy plc	940,620
Colin Ltd	535,970
Intercompany transaction	(50,000)
Total	1,426,590

(W2) COS

	£
Lucy plc	781,900
Colin Ltd	387,980
Intercompany transaction	(50,000)
Total	1,119,880

61 TROY PLC

Troy plc – Consolidated statement of financial position as at 30 June 20X9

	£000
ASSETS	
Goodwill (W1)	824
Non-current assets (17,200 + 5,000)	22,200
Current assets (W4)	7,340
	———
Total assets	30,364
	———
EQUITY AND LIABILITIES	
Equity	
Share capital	10,000
Retained earnings (W3)	5,278
Non-controlling interest (W2)	1,216
	———
Total equity	16,494
	———
Non-current liabilities (W6)	8,000
Current liabilities (W5)	5,870
	———
Total liabilities	13,870
	———
Total equity and liabilities	30,364
	———

Workings

Group share

Troy plc holding in Sherman Ltd (4,000,000/5,000,000) × 100 = 80%

NCI = 20% (100% – 80%)

(W1) Calculate goodwill

Goodwill	£000
Consideration	5,500
Net assets of Sherman Ltd at acquisition	
5,000 + 720	(5,720)
Non-controlling interest at acquisition (20% × 5,720)	1,144
Goodwill at acquisition	924
Impairment	(100)
Goodwill in SFP	824

(W2) Calculate NCI

Non-controlling interest	£000
Share capital attributable to NCI (20% × 5,000)	1,000
Retained earnings attributable to NCI (20% × 1,080)	216
Total	1,216

(W3) Retained earnings

	£000
Troy plc	5,090
Sherman Ltd post acq reserves (80% × (1,080 – 720))	288
Goodwill impairment	(100)
Total	5,278

(W4) Current assets

	£000
Troy plc	4,480
Sherman Ltd	2,860
Total	7,340

(W5) Current liabilities

	£000
Troy plc	4,590
Sherman Ltd	1,280
Total	5,870

(W6) Non-current liabilities

	£000
Troy plc	8,000
Sherman Ltd	500
Inter-company transaction	(500)
Total	8,000

62 CACTUS PLC

Cactus plc – Consolidated statement of profit or loss for the year ended 31 March 20X9

	£000
Revenue (W1)	34,900
Cost of sales (W2)	(18,675)
Gross profit	16,225
Distribution costs and administrative expenses (6,900 + 4,800 + 50 goodwill impairment)	(11,750)
Profit before tax	4,475
Income tax expense (620 + 440)	(1,060)
Profit for the year	3,415
Attributable to :	
Equity holders of Cactus plc (bal. figure)	2,994
Non-controlling interest	421
	3,415

Workings

(W1) Revenue

	£000
Cactus plc	20,500
Shore Ltd	15,200
Intercompany transaction	(800)
Total	34,900

(W2) COS

	£000
Cactus plc	11,200
Shore Ltd	8,200
Intercompany transaction	(800)
Provision for unrealised profits (W3)	75
Total	18,675

(W3) Provision for unrealised profits

	£000
Selling price	800
Cost of goods	(500)
Profit	300
Unrealised profit (300 × ¼)	75

(W4) Non-controlling interest

	£000
NCI % of Shore's profit (25% × 1,760)	440
NCI % unrealised profit (25% × 75)	(19)
Total	421

63   JACK PLC

Jack plc – Consolidated statement of financial position as at 31 March 20X9

	£000
ASSETS	
Goodwill (W1)	2,158
Non-current assets (9,400 + 3,060)	12,460
Current assets (W4)	8,550
	———
Total assets	23,168
	———
EQUITY AND LIABILITIES	
Equity	
Share capital	6,000
Retained earnings (W3)	10,493
Non-controlling interest (W2)	1,515
	———
Total equity	18,008
	———
Non-current liabilities (1,200 + 960)	2,160
Current liabilities (W5)	3,000
	———
Total liabilities	5,160
	———
Total equity and liabilities	23,168
	———

Workings

(W1) Calculate goodwill

Goodwill	£000
Consideration	5,600
Net assets of Jill Ltd at acquisition	
(4,000 + 560)	(4,560)
Non-controlling interest at acquisition (30% × 4,560)	1,368
	———
Goodwill at acquisition	2,408
Goodwill impairment	(250)
	———
Goodwill in SFP	2,158

(W2) Calculate NCI

Non-controlling interest	£000
Share capital attributable to NCI (30% × 4,000)	1,200
Retained earnings attributable to NCI (30% × 1,050*)	315
Total	1,515

*Retained earnings of Jill at year end = 1,080 – 30 after deducting the PURP (W6).

Note: We know that Jill is the selling company as it has recorded a trade receivable whilst Jack has recorded a trade payable.

(W3) Retained earnings

	£000
Jack plc	10,400
Jill Ltd post acq reserves (70% × (1,050* – 560))	343
Goodwill impairment	(250)
Total	10,493

(W4) Current assets

	£000
Jack plc	4,800
Jill Ltd	4,180
Intercompany transaction	(400)
Unrealised profit (w6)	(30)
Total	8,550

(W5) Current liabilities

	£000
Jack plc	2,200
Jill Ltd	1,200
Intercompany transaction	(400)
Total	3,000

(W6) Unrealised profit

	£000	%
Sale price	400	100
Cost (400 × 70%)	(280)	(70)
Gross profit (% on sales)	120	30

1/4 of the goods remain in inventory so the unrealised profit adjustment is £30,000 (£120,000 × 1/4). Jill sold the goods so the PURP is deducted from Jill's closing retained earnings.

64   KEN PLC

Ken plc Consolidated statement of profit or loss for the year ended 31 March 20X9

	£000
Revenue (W1)	29,460
Cost of sales (W2)	(15,605)
	————
Gross profit	13,855
Distribution costs and administrative expenses (1,250 + 800)	(2,050)
	————
Profit before tax	11,805
	————

Workings

(W1) Revenue

	£000
Ken plc	20,400
Barbie Ltd	9,300
Intercompany transaction	(240)
Total	29,460

(W2) COS

	£000
Ken plc	12,100
Barbie Ltd	3,650
Intercompany transaction	(240)
Provision for unrealised profits (W3)	95
Total	15,605

(W3) Provision for unrealised profits

	£000
Selling price	240
Cost of goods	(50)
Profit	190
Unrealised profit (190 × ½)	95

65   NORTHWOOD PLC

Goodwill at date of acquisition	
	£000
Purchase consideration	900
Net assets of Southdean Ltd at acquisition	
400 + 200 + 500	(1,100)
Non-controlling interest at acquisition (25% × 1,100)	275
Goodwill	75
Non-controlling interest at date of acquisition	
	£000
Share capital acquired (25% × £400,000)	100
Share premium acquired (25% × £200,000)	50
Retained earnings acquired (25% × £500,000)	125
NCI at acquisition	275

66   TOWERHILL GROUP

Consolidated statement of profit or loss for the year ended 31 December 20X5.

	£000
Continuing operations	
Revenue (W1)	926
Cost of sales (W2)	(472)
Gross profit	454
Other income (W4)	110
Distribution costs (W5)	(105)
Administrative expenses (W6)	(65)
Profit from operations	394
Finance costs (W7)	(35)
Profit before tax	359
Tax (W8)	(75)
Profit for the year from continuing operations	284
Attributable to:	
Equity holders of the parent (bal fig)	249
Non-controlling interest (25% × £140)	35
	284

Workings

(W1) Revenue

	£000
T plc	500
W Ltd	450
Interco sale	(24)
	926

(W2) Cost of sales

	£000
T plc	275
W Ltd	220
Interco purchase	(24)
PUP adjust (W3)	1
	472

(W3) PUP working

	£000	
Selling price	24	
Cost of goods sold	20	
Profit	4	
PUP adjust	1	(¼ × £4,000)
One quarter of the goods sold, remain in inventory at the year end.		

(W4) Other income

	£000
T plc	80
W Ltd	40
Divi from W Ltd	(10)
	110

(W5) Distribution costs

	£000
T plc	60
W Ltd	45
	105

(W6) Administrative expenses

	£000
T plc	30
W Ltd	35
	———
	65
	———

(W7) Finance costs

	£000
T plc	20
W Ltd	15
	———
	35
	———

(W8) Tax expense

	£000
T plc	40
W Ltd	35
	———
	75
	———

ANALYSIS AND INTERPRETATION OF FINANCIAL STATEMENTS (FORMULAS AND CALCULATIONS)

67   PAREK LTD

		20X1	
Gross profit percentage		**Working £000**	**Answer**
$\dfrac{\text{Gross profit}}{\text{Revenue}} \times 100$		$\dfrac{19{,}245}{39{,}680} \times 100$	= 48.5%
Operating profit percentage			
$\dfrac{\text{Operating profit}}{\text{Revenue}} \times 100$		$\dfrac{3{,}175}{39{,}680} \times 100$	= 8.0%
Return on capital employed			
$\dfrac{\text{Profit from operations}}{\text{Equity} + \text{non-current liabilities}} \times 100$		$\dfrac{3175}{31530 + 3000} \times 100$	= 9.2%
Current ratio			
$\dfrac{\text{Current assets}}{\text{Current liabilities}}$		$\dfrac{8{,}670}{3{,}260}$	= 2.66:1

Trade receivable collection period		
$\dfrac{\text{Trade receivables}}{\text{Revenue}} \times 365$	$\dfrac{3{,}712}{39{,}680} \times 365$	= 34.1 days
Trade payables payment period		
$\dfrac{\text{Trade payables}}{\text{Cost of sales}} \times 365$	$\dfrac{1{,}675}{20{,}435} \times 365$	= 29.9 days
Gearing ratio		
$\dfrac{\text{Non-current liabilities}}{\text{Total equity + non-current liabilities}} \times 100$	$\dfrac{3{,}000}{31{,}530 + 3{,}000} \times 100$	= 8.7%

68 REGENCY LTD

	20X1	
Gross profit percentage	**Working £000**	**Answer**
$\dfrac{\text{Gross profit}}{\text{Revenue}} \times 100$	$\dfrac{19{,}224}{37{,}920} \times 100$	= 50.7%
Expenses/revenue percentage		
$\dfrac{\text{Expenses}}{\text{Revenue}} \times 100$	$\dfrac{9{,}220 + 4{,}782}{37{,}920} \times 100$	= 36.9%
Return on shareholders' funds		
$\dfrac{\text{Profit after tax}}{\text{Equity}} \times 100$	$\dfrac{3{,}380}{22{,}626} \times 100$	= 14.9%
Current ratio		
$\dfrac{\text{Current assets}}{\text{Current liabilities}}$	$\dfrac{7{,}852}{4{,}826}$	= 1.6:1
Acid test ratio		
$\dfrac{\text{Current assets} - \text{inventories}}{\text{Current liabilities}}$	$\dfrac{7{,}852 - 1{,}872}{4{,}826}$	= 1.2:1
Trade receivable collection period		
$\dfrac{\text{Trade receivables}}{\text{Revenue}} \times 365$	$\dfrac{3{,}795}{37{,}920} \times 365$	= 36.5 days
Trade payables payment period		
$\dfrac{\text{Trade payables}}{\text{Cost of sales}} \times 365$	$\dfrac{3{,}513}{18{,}696} \times 365$	= 68.6 days
Gearing ratio		
$\dfrac{\text{Non-current liabilities}}{\text{Total equity + non-current liabilities}} \times 100$	$\dfrac{5{,}000}{22{,}626 + 5{,}000} \times 100$	= 18.1%

69 ARCTIC FOX LTD

	20X1	
Gross profit percentage	**Working £000**	**Answer**
$\dfrac{\text{Gross profit}}{\text{Revenue}} \times 100$	$\dfrac{2,500}{20,500} \times 100$	= 12.2%
Asset turnover (net assets)		
$\dfrac{\text{Revenue}}{\text{Total assets} - \text{current liabilities}}$	$\dfrac{20,500}{13,100 - 4,000}$	= 2.25
Return on capital employed		
$\dfrac{\text{Profit from operations}}{\text{Equity} + \text{non-current liabilities}} \times 100$	$\dfrac{1,990}{2,800 + 6,300} \times 100$	= 21.9%
Current ratio		
$\dfrac{\text{Current assets}}{\text{Current liabilities}}$	$\dfrac{7,300}{4,000}$	= 1.8:1
Acid test ratio		
$\dfrac{\text{Current assets} - \text{inventories}}{\text{Current liabilities}}$	$\dfrac{3,700}{4,000}$	= 0.9:1
Trade payables collection period		
$\dfrac{\text{Trade payables}}{\text{Cost of sales}} \times 365$	$\dfrac{3,800}{18,000} \times 365$	= 77 days
Inventory holding period (days)		
$\dfrac{\text{Inventories}}{\text{Cost of sales}} \times 365$	$\dfrac{3,600}{18,000} \times 365$	= 73 days
Gearing ratio		
$\dfrac{\text{Non-current liabilities}}{\text{Total equity} + \text{non-current liabilities}} \times 100$	$\dfrac{6,300}{2,800 + 6,300} \times 100$	= 69.2%
Interest cover		
$\dfrac{\text{Operating profit}}{\text{Finance costs}}$	$\dfrac{1,990}{590}$	= 3.4 times

70   SHIELD LTD

	20X9	
Gross profit percentage	**Working £000**	**Answer**
$\dfrac{\text{Gross profit}}{\text{Revenue}} \times 100$	$\dfrac{16{,}400}{45{,}700} \times 100$	= 35.9%
Operating profit percentage		
$\dfrac{\text{Operating profit}}{\text{Revenue}} \times 100$	$\dfrac{6{,}256}{45{,}700} \times 100$	= 13.7%
Current ratio		
$\dfrac{\text{Current assets}}{\text{Current liabilities}}$	$\dfrac{7{,}010}{9{,}398}$	= 0.7:1
Acid test ratio		
$\dfrac{\text{Current assets} - \text{inventories}}{\text{Current liabilities}}$	$\dfrac{7{,}010 - 2{,}220}{9{,}398}$	= 0.5:1
Trade receivable collection period		
$\dfrac{\text{Trade receivables}}{\text{Revenue}} \times 365$	$\dfrac{3{,}970}{45{,}700} \times 365$	= 31.7 days
Inventory turnover		
$\dfrac{\text{Cost of sales}}{\text{Inventory}}$	$\dfrac{29{,}300}{2{,}220}$	= 13.2
Gearing ratio		
$\dfrac{\text{Non-current liabilities}}{\text{Total equity} + \text{non-current liabilities}} \times 100$	$\dfrac{6{,}000}{27{,}312 + 6{,}000} \times 100$	= 18.0%

71 SUGAR AND SPICE LTD

	20X9	
Asset turnover (net assets)	**Working £000**	**Answer**
$$\dfrac{\text{Revenue}}{\text{Total assets} - \text{current liabilities}}$$	$$\dfrac{74,400}{70,860 - 7,224}$$	= 1.17
Operating profit percentage		
$$\dfrac{\text{Operating profit}}{\text{Revenue}} \times 100$$	$$\dfrac{5,952}{74,400} \times 100$$	= 8.0%
Return on capital employed		
$$\dfrac{\text{Profit from operations}}{\text{Equity} + \text{non-current liabilities}} \times 100$$	$$\dfrac{5,952}{57,636 + 6,000} \times 100$$	= 9.4%
Current ratio		
$$\dfrac{\text{Current assets}}{\text{Current liabilities}}$$	$$\dfrac{16,260}{7,224}$$	= 2.3:1
Acid test ratio		
$$\dfrac{\text{Current assets} - \text{inventories}}{\text{Current liabilities}}$$	$$\dfrac{16,260 - 3,780}{7,224}$$	= 1.7:1
Trade receivable collection period		
$$\dfrac{\text{Trade receivables}}{\text{Revenue}} \times 365$$	$$\dfrac{6,960}{74,400} \times 365$$	= 34.1 days
Inventory holding period (days)		
$$\dfrac{\text{Inventories}}{\text{Cost of sales}} \times 365$$	$$\dfrac{3,780}{38,316} \times 365$$	= 36.0 days
Gearing ratio		
$$\dfrac{\text{Non-current liabilities}}{\text{Total equity} + \text{non-current liabilities}} \times 100$$	$$\dfrac{6,000}{57,636 + 6,000} \times 100$$	= 9.4%

72 HIGHTOWN LTD

Calculation of ratios

Return on capital employed	$\dfrac{\text{Profit from operations}}{\text{Equity + non-current liabilities}} \times 100$	$\dfrac{5,344}{9,000 + 1,000} \times 100$	53.4%
Interest cover	$\dfrac{\text{Operating profit}}{\text{Finance costs}}$	$\dfrac{5,344}{60}$	89.0 times
Current ratio	$\dfrac{\text{Current assets}}{\text{Current liabilities}} : 1$	$\dfrac{6,215}{5,540}$	1.1:1
Operating profit percentage	$\dfrac{\text{Operating profit}}{\text{Revenue}} \times 100$	$\dfrac{5,344}{23,750} \times 100\%$	22.5%
Inventory holding period (days)	$\dfrac{\text{Inventories}}{\text{Cost of sales}} \times 365 \text{ days}$	$\dfrac{2,446}{12,231} \times 365$	73 days

ANALYSIS AND INTERPRETATION OF FINANCIAL STATEMENTS (WRITTEN ELEMENT)

73 CHILLED LTD

(a) **Comment on the relative performance of the company for the two years and what this tells you about the company:**

Report

To:	Michael Davies
From:	AAT student
Subject:	Analysis of Chilled Ltd
Date:	xx/xx/xxxx

As requested I have looked into the financial situation of Chilled Ltd.

(i) The **gross profit ratio** has improved.

More gross profit is being generated by sales/gross profit margin on sales.

Improvement may be due to increasing sales price or decreasing the cost of sales or both. There could have been a change in the product mix.

(ii) The **operating profit ratio** has deteriorated.

Less operating profit is being generated from sales.

This could be due to either a decrease in the sales margins or an increase in expenses, or both.

As the gross margins have improved, it must be the result of an increase in expenses.

(iii)   The **return on capital employed** has deteriorated.

Less net profit is being generated from the level of capital employed.

(iv)   The **gearing ratio** has deteriorated.

This could cause problems obtaining loans in the future.

The company will appear to be more risky.

The ratio would have deteriorated if the company has taken out additional loans during the year.

(v)   The **interest cover ratio** has deteriorated.

There is now less operating profit to cover interest payments.

The company will appear more risky.

The ratio deterioration could be caused by lower operating profits/higher interest payments.

Higher interest payments could be due to new loans taken out during the year.

(b)   A conclusion advising Michael on advising the board:

The gross profit margin has increased but the operating profit is falling. The company therefore needs to look at its operating costs and to control these much better, which would then improve the interest cover and make the company less risky. They should also look at the financing structure of the company and try and improve the gearing ratio.

74   WESTELLA LTD

(a)   Comment on the relative performance of the company for the two years and what this tells you about the company:

Report

To: Claire Jones

From: AAT Student

Subject: Investment in Westella Ltd

Date:

As requested I have looked into the financial situation of Westella Ltd.

Gross profit

The gross profit ratio has improved by 2.5% from the previous year. A higher gross profit has been generated in 20X1 either from increasing the sales price or by reducing the cost of sales or all of these.

This could also have been from a change in the product mix.

Operating profit

The operating profit has reduced by 3.5% from the previous year, which means that less operating profit is being generated from sales.

This could be a result of an increase in either distribution costs or administration costs, for example; an increase in fuel prices. More information would be required to try to establish why the costs have increased.

Gearing ratio

The gearing ratio has deteriorated by 8.94%.

This means that the company is more highly geared since the previous year and this could be due to the company raising money via loans. If this is the case it shows a positive side that the bank is still willing to lend money to the company. It could cause problems in the future if Westella needs to borrow additional funds as the company will be deemed to be more risky.

Quick ratio

This has deteriorated to below 1:1, which is usually considered to be the safe threshold. This means that Westella cannot repay its short term debt. This could be particularly problematic if it has a short term overdraft or tax liabilities. If it cannot repay these then Westella may be put into administration.

This could be a result of the falling operating margin.

Return on equity/shareholders' funds

This has fallen during the year. It could be due to an increase in equity balances, for example; due to a share issue. It is more likely, however, that this is due to the deteriorating margins. This, in combination with the poor liquidity, may cause concern for shareholders, who may believe that this will impact future dividends.

(b)   Conclusion

Claire should be advised to seriously consider her investment in the company as the investment is potentially looking risky as overall profitability has deteriorated and short term liquidity is poor.

75   CALIFORNIA LTD

(a)   Comment on the relative performance of the company for the two years and what this tells you about the company:

Report

To:	Daisy Duke
From:	AAT student
Subject:	Possible investment in California Ltd
Date:	1 July 20X9

As requested I have looked into the financial situation of California Ltd.

(i)   The **gross profit ratio** has improved.

More gross profit is being generated by sales.

Improvement may be due to increasing the sales price per unit or decreasing the cost of sales or both. This could also be due to a change in the product mix or a new supplier contract.

(ii)   The **return on equity/shareholders' funds** has improved.

More net profit is being generated from the equity invested in the company.

This is most likely due to an increase in reported profits in the current year without any increases in share capital.

(iii)   Inventory **turnover** has risen.

This indicates that either sales are growing and inventory levels are being maintained at a stable rate or that the business is managing inventory more effectively and has managed to improve overall inventory levels.

Either way, more effective inventory management reduces the costs associated with holding inventory and this could be one of the reasons for the improvements in profitability reported above.

(iv)   The **interest cover ratio** has improved.

This indicates that California is better able to pay its interest commitments. This reduces the risk profile of the business and is either the result of the improvement in profits or a reduction in loan commitments.

(b)   A conclusion advising Daisy whether or not to invest:

Daisy should be advised to invest since profitability has improved and the business appears to be more efficient. The business also appears to be more attractive to investors as both EPS and interest cover are improving.

76   JOHN LTD

(a)   Comment on the relative performance of the company for the two years and what this tells you about the company:

Report

To:	Tina Campbell
From:	AAT student
Subject:	Possible investment in John Ltd
Date:	18 June 20X1

As requested I have looked into the financial situation of John Ltd.

(i)   The **operating profit ratio** has deteriorated.

This may indicate that operating expenses have increased significantly, such as fuel costs.

Alternatively, sales may be falling and John Ltd is unable to adjust expenses to reflect the decline, for example: rent and staff costs may be (relatively) fixed.

(ii)   The **return on capital employed** has deteriorated.

This may be due to the overall reduction in profitability of the business, which is generating less profit off its asset base.

It could also be because of an investment in new capital assets in an attempt to improve revenues and profits in the future.

(iii) The **trade receivables collection period** has lengthened.

John Ltd are taking longer to collect cash off credit customers. This could be a marketing strategy to attract new customers or it could be due to a deterioration in credit control.

Either way, the costs of holding receivables will undoubtedly increase due to the cost of administering them and the risks of irrecoverable debt.

(iv)   The **trade payables period** has shortened.

It is possible that John Ltd is paying suppliers quicker to earn prompt payment discounts.

However, to maximise cash flows John Ltd should retain the cash in their own accounts as long as possible (without upsetting suppliers). Coupled with the increased receivables collection period this will lead to worse cash flow for John Ltd.

(v)   The **gearing ratio** has deteriorated, indicating that more loans have been taken out during the year.

There has been a significant increase in gearing, which indicates significant new loan finance. Whilst this will be put to use within the business it will lead to increases in finance charges, which will further reduce profitability in the future. It will also increase the risk profile of John Ltd for potential investors.

(b)   A conclusion advising Tina whether or not to invest:

Tina should be advised **not to invest** since profitability has deteriorated, cash flows would appear to have deteriorated and the business is more risky from an investor's perspective.

77   CHAN LTD

(a)   Comment on the working capital management of Chan Ltd for the two years ended 31 December 20X9, giving possible reasons for the change in performance from 20X8 to 20X9.

Inventory holding period

The inventory holding period has fallen from 20X8 to 20X9. This is normally an indication of improved inventory management as goods are held in inventory for a shorter time period between purchase or production of goods and their sale to customers.

One reason for the improvement could be that Chan Ltd is focussing upon purchasing or producing only those goods which it knows it can sell to customers.

Another reason for the improvement could be that Chan Ltd has written off and disposed of slow-moving or obsolete goods from inventory. This would result in inventory consisting only of those goods which can be sold and will therefore reduce the average holding period for items in inventory.

Trade receivables collection period

The trade receivables collection period has fallen from 45 days to 40 days, meaning that Chan Ltd collected cash from customers more quickly than it did during 20X8.

This will benefit the business as it will reduce the time and cost of following up customers to obtain payment and potentially reduce bank charges and interest costs.

One reason this may have happened is that Chan Ltd may have introduced more effective credit management procedures before they authorise credit sales to particular customers.

Linked with this, Chan Ltd may be more effective at enforcing the credit terms agreed with customers.

Another possibility is that Chan Ltd has introduced a scheme to permit prompt payment discounts to those customers who pay their outstanding invoices within a specified period of time.

Trade payables payment period

The trade creditors' payment period has been increased from 30 to 35 days. This could be considered as beneficial to Chan Ltd as the company is using credit from suppliers to finance the business.

It may be that the extension of the payment period has been agreed with suppliers, especially if Chan Ltd is a major customer who can enforce better terms of business with their suppliers. Equally, suppliers may be happy to do this if they expect that it will lead to increased business and more sales with Chan Ltd in future.

Alternatively, it could be that the trade payables payment period has increased because Chan Ltd is unable to meet the credit terms agreed with suppliers. If this was the case, Chan Ltd would be at risk of suppliers refusing to make further sales unless they agreed to comply with their agreed terms of business.

Working capital cycle

The working capital cycle represents the time period between payment for inventory and receipt of cash from customers for the sale of goods or services. Ideally, this time period should be as short as possible.

The working capital cycle has reduced to 31 days in 20X9 in comparison with 45 days in 20X8. This means that the business is managing working capital more effectively in 20X9 and the time period between paying for inventory and recovering that outlay from cash received from customers has reduced by 14 days. This is a significant improvement.

Based upon the previous comments, this has occurred as a result of the extension of the credit period taken from suppliers, whilst managing to obtain prompt payment from customers.

(b) **Explain why financial ratios calculated using historic financial information may not always be a good basis for predicting future financial performance.**

Financial ratios are often calculated using historic information, such as the working capital ratios for the years ended 20X9 and 20X8 used in part (a) part of this question.

Whilst it may be possible that past financial performance may be a useful guide to what future financial performance may be expected, it is not a guarantee. There are many factors why future financial performance may be different to that achieved in the past (some the business can control or others outside of the control of the business), such as:

*   The company changing its business strategy to attract more sales e.g. reduce prices to be more competitive. This will reduce the gross profit margin.

*   The company may increase levels of inventory to support seasonal sales (e.g. Christmas products) or to support a sales or marketing campaign later in the year. This will change the inventory holding period.

*   Changes in law or regulation, such as more stringent electrical safety standards may increase product costs and reduce profitability.

*   Changes in taxation policy or tax rates may also affect the selling price of products and therefore demand for those products – such as the price of tobacco and alcohol products.

*   The business strategies of competitors and suppliers will also have an impact upon the purchases, sales and profitability and liquidity of a business.

Section 3

MOCK ASSESSMENT QUESTIONS

TASK 1   **(23 MARKS)**

You have been asked to help prepare the financial statements of Wolf Ltd for the year ended 31 March 20X6. The company's trial balance as at 31 March 20X6 is shown below.

Wolf Ltd

Trial balance as at 31 March 20X6

	Debit £	Credit £
Sales		72,813
Purchases	35,108	
Inventories as at 1 April 20X5	12,572	
Final dividend paid for year end 31 March 20X5	1,000	
Interim dividend paid for year end 31 March 20X6	600	
Interest	700	
Distribution costs	12,533	
Administrative expenses	9,311	
Trade receivables	9,122	
Cash at bank	473	
7% debentures		20,000
Ordinary share capital		10,000
Share premium		8,000
Retained earnings		17,349
Trade payables		2,927
Accruals		412
Property, plant and equipment – cost	71,338	
Property, plant and equipment – accumulated depreciation		21,256
	152,757	152,757

Further information:

(i)   The issued ordinary share capital of the company consists of ordinary shares with a nominal value of 25p.

(ii)   Inventories at the close of business on 31 March 20X6 cost £14,186.

(iii)   The corporation tax charge for the year has been calculated as £3,537.

(iv)   Interest on the debentures for the last six months of the year has not been included in the accounts in the trial balance.

(v)   Land included in Property, plant and equipment at a carrying amount of £24,000 is to be revalued at the end of the year to £29,000.

All of the operations are continuing operations.

(a)   Draft the statement of profit or loss and other comprehensive income of Wolf Ltd for the year ended 31 March 20X6.   (18 marks)

Note: Additional notes and disclosures are not required, you should present your answers to the nearest £.

Wolf Ltd – Statement of profit or loss and other comprehensive income for the year ended 31 March 20X6

	£
Revenue	
Cost of sales	————
Gross profit	
Distribution costs	
Administrative expenses	————
Profit from operations	
Finance costs	————
Profit before tax	
Tax	————
Profit for the period	
Other comprehensive income for the year	
	————
Total comprehensive income for the year	
	————

Workings

(W1)

Cost of sales	£
	————
Total COS	
	————

(W2)

Finance costs	£
	_____
Statement of profit or loss charge	
	_____

(W3)

Land	£
	_____
Revaluation of land	
	_____

Workings drop down

Cost of sales: Marketing costs/Irrecoverable debt/Closing inventories/Opening inventories/Purchases/Purchase returns/Sales/Sales returns

Finance costs: marketing costs/irrecoverable debt/misclassified salary/sales returns/purchases returns/sales/interest/interest accrued

Land: carrying amount/revalued amount

(b) **Draft a statement of changes in equity for Wolf Ltd for the year ended 31 March 20X6.**

(5 marks)

Statement of changes in equity

	Share capital	Share premium	Revaluation surplus	Retained earnings	Total
	£	£	£	£	£
Bal b/f					
Total comprehensive income					
Dividends					
Bal c/f					

TASK 2 (17 MARKS)

This task is a continuation of task 1 and uses the same data.

Draft the statement of financial position for Wolf Ltd as at 31 March 20X6.

Note: Additional notes and disclosures are not required, you should present your answers to the nearest £.

Wolf Ltd – Statement of financial position as at 31 March 20X6

	£000
ASSETS	
Non-current assets	
	_____
Current assets	
	_____
	_____
Total assets	_____
EQUITY AND LIABILITIES	
Equity	
Total equity	
Non-current liabilities	
Current liabilities	
Total liabilities	
Total equity and liabilities	

Drop downs:

Bank loan/Cash and cash equivalents/Inventories/Property, plant and equipment/Retained earnings/Revaluation surplus/Share capital/Share premium/Tax liability/Trade and other payables/Trade receivables/7% Debentures

Workings

(W1)

PPE	£000
	_____
Total PPE @ CA	_____

(W2)

	Retained earnings £	Revaluation surplus £
Opening balance		
	————	————
Closing balance		
	————	————

(W3)

Trade and other payables	£
	————
Total trade and other payables	
	————

Workings drop downs

PPE: Plant and equipment cost/Accumulated depreciation/Depreciation charge/Revaluation of land

Retained earnings and revaluation surplus: Opening balance/Profit for the period/Share capital/Share premium/Dividends paid/Revaluation

Trade and other payables: Trade payables/Interest accrued/Accruals/Receivables/Interest

TASK 3 (8 MARKS)

(a) Define the following elements of financial statements:

   (i)   Assets

   (ii)   Liabilities (2 marks)

(b) Explain why inventories are an asset of a company based on the IFRS Conceptual Framework (2018). (4 marks)

(c) Identify whether each of the following statements is true or false in relation to reporting frameworks. (2 marks)

	True	False
All businesses must follow the International Financial Reporting Standards (IFRS) when preparing their financial statements.		
Based on the IFRS Conceptual Framework (2018), faithful representation is one of the 'fundamental' characteristics.		

TASK 4 (12 MARKS)

Data

The year end for Min plc is 31 March 20X6.

On 21st April 20X6 there was a fire at the company's premises that destroyed Property, plant and equipment and inventories. The losses from the fire amounted to £487,000 and they were not covered by the company's insurance policy. The amount is considered by the directors of Min plc to constitute a material loss to the company.

(a) **Prepare brief notes for the directors of Min plc to answer the following questions:**

    (i) **Explain what is meant by 'events after the reporting period' per IAS 10.** **(2 marks)**

    (ii) **Distinguish between events after the reporting date that are adjusting events and those that are non-adjusting events.** **(2 marks)**

    (iii) **Explain how you would treat the losses that arose from the fire on the company's premises on 21 April 20X6.** **(2 marks)**

Stubbs Ltd sells kitchen and dining furniture and has a year end of 31 December 20X1. The items are sold via its stores and also its website. In December 20X1 the company received deposits of £35,000 for orders totalling £130,000. The goods relating to these orders were delivered to the customers in January 20X1.

(b) **Select the amount of revenue that should be recognised in the financial statements of Stubbs Ltd for the year ended 31 December 20X1 in relation to these orders.** **(2 marks)**

	£
£0	
£35,000	
£130,000	

Stubbs Ltd has an item of machinery used to make kitchen chairs, which unfortunately has produced fewer units this year than had been expected. The machine has a carrying value of £25,000. The company has identified the value in use of the machine as £18,750 and determined that the machine can be sold for £21,500 (net of selling costs).

(c) **(i)** **Select the amount at which the machine should be recognised in the financial statements.** **(2 marks)**

	£
£18,750	
£21,500	
£25,000	

    (ii) **Explain your answer to part (i).** **(2 marks)**

TASK 5   **(30 MARKS)**

Data

On 1 April 20X5 Alasmith plc acquired 60% of the issued share capital of Jones Ltd for £26,680,000. At that date Jones Ltd had retained earnings of £19,800,000.

Extracts of the statements of financial position for the companies at 31 March 20X6 are as follows:

	Alasmith plc £000	Jones Ltd £000
NON-CURRENT ASSETS		
Property, plant and equipment	56,320	39,320
Investment in Jones Ltd	26,680	
	83,000	39,320
Current assets		
Inventories	13,638	5,470
Trade and other receivables	7,839	3,218
Cash and cash equivalents	1,013	1,184
	22,490	9,872
Total assets	105,490	49,192
EQUITY AND LIABILITIES		
Equity		
Share capital	25,000	6,000
Share premium	10,000	4,000
Retained earnings	40,248	25,200
Total equity	75,248	35,200
Non-current liabilities		
Long term loan	20,000	8,850
Current liabilities		
Trade and other payables	9,183	4,831
Tax	1,059	311
Total liabilities	30,242	13,992
Total equity and liabilities	105,490	49,192

Additional data:

1   Buildings in Jones Ltd at 1 April 20X5 was carried at £35,470,000 but had a fair value of £43,470,000. This has not yet been reflected in the books of Jones Ltd.

2   Non-controlling interests are to be valued at their proportionate share of net assets. Goodwill is to be impaired by 10%.

Draft the consolidated statement of financial position for Alasmith plc and its subsidiary undertaking as at 31 March 20X6.

Your calculations should work to the nearest £000.

Alasmith plc – Consolidated statement of financial position as at 31 March 20X6

	£000
ASSETS	
	_____
	_____
Current assets	
	_____
	_____
Total assets	_____
EQUITY AND LIABILITIES	
Equity	
	_____
Total equity	_____
Non-current liabilities	
	_____
Current liabilities	
	_____
Total liabilities	_____
Total equity and liabilities	_____

Workings

(W1) Goodwill

	£000
Goodwill in SFP	

(W2) NCI

	£000
NCI	

(W3) Retained earnings

	£000
Group retained earnings	

Working drop downs

Goodwill: Consideration/Impairment/Net assets at acquisition/Non-controlling interest at acquisition/Jones Ltd – post-acquisition profits attributable to Alasmith plc

NCI: Retained earnings/Share capital acquired/Share premium acquired/Impairment/Fair value adjustment

Retained earnings: Impairment/Alasmith plc/Jones Ltd – post-acquisition profits attributable to Alasmith plc/Net assets at acquisition

TASK 6 (8 MARKS)

Data

Madge Keygone is the managing director of Asbeen Ltd. She has just returned from a meeting with one of the major shareholders of the company.

The shareholder was concerned about the current ratio, acid test ratio, inventories holding period and trade receivables collection period and how they compare with the industry averages.

Madge did not understand the shareholders concern and asked you to help her.

She has given you the summarised financial statements of Asbeen Ltd and has obtained the industry averages for these ratios from computerised databases.

Asbeen Ltd – Statement of profit or loss and other comprehensive income for the year ended 31 March 20X6

	20X6
	£000
Revenue	14,994
Cost of sales	(8,716)
	———
Gross profit	6,278
Distribution costs	(2,037)
Administrative expenses	(1,541)
	———
Profit from operations	2,700
Finance costs	(274)
	———
Profit before tax	2,426
Tax	(631)
	———
Profit for the period	1,795
	———

Asbeen Ltd – Statement of financial position as at 31 March 20X6

	£000
ASSETS	
Non-current assets	
Property, plant and equipment	11,432
Current assets	
Inventories	4,200
Trade receivables	2,095
Cash and cash equivalents	145
	6,440
Total assets	17,872
EQUITY AND LIABILITIES	
Equity	
Share capital	5,000
Retained earnings	5,572
Total equity	10,572
Non-current liabilities	
Bank loans	4,500
	4,500
Current liabilities	
Trade payables	2,169
Tax liabilities	631
	2,800
Total liabilities	7,300
Total equity and liabilities	17,872

Calculate the following ratios to ONE decimal place. **(8 marks)**

Quick ratio		:1
Inventories holding period (days)		days
Trade receivables collection period (days)		days
Interest cover		times

TASK 7   **(22 MARKS)**

Coleen Best is considering buying shares in Manity Ltd and has asked you to assist her in determining the level of profitability and risk of the company. You have computed the following ratios in respect of Manity Ltd's financial statements for the last two years to assist you in your analysis.

	20X1	20X0
Gross profit percentage	38.0%	32.0%
Expenses/revenue	18.5%	20%
Return on equity/shareholders' funds	11.4%	9.8%
Gearing	31.8%	27.9%
Current ratio	2:1	1.9:1

(a)   **For EACH of the ratios given above:**

    (i)   **Identify whether the ratio is better or worse compared to the previous year.**

                                            (5 marks)

    (ii)   **Explain what this may tell you about the company.**   **(15 marks)**

(b)   **Recommend, with reasons based on the ratios you have calculated, on whether or not Coleen should invest.**   **(2 marks)**

Section 4

MOCK ASSESSMENT ANSWERS

TASK 1 **(23 MARKS)**

(a) **Wolf Ltd – Statement of profit or loss and other comprehensive income for the year ended 31 March 20X6** **(18 marks)**

	£
Revenue	72,813
Cost of sales (W1)	(33,494)
	————
Gross profit	39,319
Distribution costs	(12,533)
Administrative expenses	(9,311)
	————
Profit from operations	17,475
Finance costs (W2)	(1,400)
	————
Profit before tax	16,075
Tax	(3,537)
	————
Profit for the period	12,538
Other comprehensive income for the year	
Revaluation surplus – land (W3)	5,000
	————
Total comprehensive income for the year	17,538
	————

Workings

(W1)

Cost of sales	£
Opening inventories	12,572
Purchases	35,108
Closing inventories	(14,186)
	————
Total COS	33,494
	————

(W2)

	£
Finance costs	
Interest paid per trial balance	700
Interest accrued (7% × 20,000 = 1,400 per year. Six months to accrue = 700)	700
	———
Statement of profit or loss charge	1,400
	———

(W3)

	£
Carrying amount	24,000
Revalued amount	29,000
	———
Revaluation surplus	5,000

(b) **Draft a statement of changes in equity for Wolf Ltd for the year ended 31 March 20X6.**

(5 marks)

Statement of changes in equity

	Share capital	Share premium	Revaluation surplus	Retained earnings	Total
	£	£	£	£	£
Bal b/f	10,000	8,000	0	17,349	35,349
Total comprehensive income			5,000	12,538	17,538
Dividends				(1,600)	(1,600)
Bal c/f	10,000	8,000	5,000	28,287	51,287

TASK 2

(17 MARKS)

Wolf Ltd – Statement of financial position as at 31 March 20X1

	£000
ASSETS	
Non-current assets	
Property, plant and equipment (W1)	55,082
	———
Current assets	
Inventories	14,186
Trade receivables	9,122
Cash and cash equivalents	473
	———
	23,781
	———
Total assets	78,863
	———

EQUITY AND LIABILITIES

Equity

Share capital	10,000
Share premium	8,000
Revaluation surplus (W2)	5,000
Retained earnings (W2)	28,287
Total equity	**51,287**

Non-current liabilities

7% Debentures	20,000

Current liabilities

Trade and other payables (W3)	4,039
Tax liability	3,537
	7,576
Total liabilities	**27,576**
Total equity and liabilities	**78,863**

Workings

(W1)

	£
Property, plant and equipment	
Plant and equipment @cost	71,338
Revaluation of land	5,000
Accumulated depreciation	(21,256)
Total PPE @ CA	55,082

(W2)

	Retained earnings	Revaluation surplus
	£	£
Opening balance	17,349	0
Revaluation	–	5,000
Profit for the period	12,538	
Dividends paid (1,000 + 600)	(1,600)	
Closing balance	28,287	5,000

(W3)

Trade and other payables	£
Trade payables per trial balance	2,927
Interest accrued	700
Accruals (TB)	412
	———
Total trade and other payables	4,039
	———

TASK 3 (8 MARKS)

1   The elements of financial statements are defined by the *Conceptual Framework for Financial Reporting (the Framework)* as follows:

(i)   'An asset is a present economic resource controlled by an entity as a result of a past event. An economic resource is a right that has the potential to produce economic benefit.'

(ii) 'A liability is a present obligation of the entity to transfer an economic resource as a result of a past event.'   **(2 marks)**

2   Inventories meet the definition of an asset in that:

- The purchase/manufacture of inventories is a past event. The inventory is owned and therefore controlled by the company who purchased/manufactured it.

- The inventories have the potential to produce economic benefits because Wolf Ltd can sell the inventories to generate cash.   **(4 marks)**

3

	True	False
All businesses must follow the International Financial Reporting Standards (IFRS) when preparing their financial statements.		✓
Based on the IFRS Conceptual Framework (2018), faithful representation is one of the 'fundamental' characteristics.	✓	

Only companies are required to prepare their financial statements in line with a set of financial reporting standards. Sole traders and partnerships do not have to follow the standards. Companies in the UK may use IFRS or UK accounting standards.   **(2 marks)**

TASK 4 (12 MARKS)

(a) **Prepare brief notes for the directors of Min plc to answer the following questions:**

(i) **Explain what is meant by 'events after the reporting period per IAS 10'**

IAS 10 says that events after the reporting period are events, 'favourable and unfavourable, that occur between the statement of financial position date and the date when the financial statements are authorised for issue.' [IAS 10, para 3]   (2 marks)

(ii) **Distinguish between events after the reporting date that are adjusting events and ones that are non-adjusting events.**

Adjusting events are those events 'that provide additional evidence of conditions that existed at the statement of financial position date'. Non-adjusting events are those events 'that are indicative of conditions that arose after the statement of financial position date.' [IAS 10, para 3]   (2 marks)

(iii) **Explain how you would treat the losses that arose from the fire on the company's premises on 21 April 20X6.**

The losses that arose from the fire on the company's premises on 21 April 20X6 constitute a 'non-adjusting' event. The condition did not exist at the statement of financial position date, but came into existence after that date. No adjustment is required for the event as the conditions did not exist at the statement of financial position date.

However, if the event is so material that non-disclosure could influence the economic decisions of users taken on the basis of the financial statements then the entity should disclose the nature of the event and an estimate of its financial effect, or a statement that such an estimate cannot be made, by way of a note to the accounts.   (2 marks)

(b) **Select the amount of revenue that should be recognised in the financial statements of Stubbs Ltd for the year ended 31 December 20X1.**   (2 marks)

	£
£0	✓
£35,000	
£130,000	

(c) (i) **Select the amount at which the machine should be recognised in the financial statements.**   (2 marks)

	£
£18,750	
£21,500	✓
£25,000	

(ii) The fact that the machine is producing fewer units this year is an indication that the asset is impaired. An impairment review should therefore be performed, by comparing the carrying amount of the asset to its recoverable amount.

The recoverable amount is determined by taking the higher of the value in use of £18,750 and fair value less costs to sell of £21,500, hence the recoverable amount is £21,500. This is below the carrying amount, so the asset should be written down to £21,500 and an impairment expense of £3,500 (£25,000 – £21,500) should be recognised in the statement of profit or loss.   (2 marks)

TASK 5 (30 MARKS)

Alasmith plc – Consolidated statement of financial position as at 31 March 20X6

	£000
ASSETS	
Goodwill (W1)	3,600
Property, plant and equipment (56,320 + 39,320 + 8,000)	103,640
	107,240
Current assets	
Inventories (13,638 + 5,470)	19,108
Trade and other receivables (7,839 + 3,218)	11,057
Cash and cash equivalents (1,013 + 1,184)	2,197
	32,362
Total assets	139,602
EQUITY AND LIABILITIES	
Equity	
Share capital	25,000
Share premium account	10,000
Retained earnings (W3)	43,088
Non-controlling interest (W2)	17,280
Total equity	95,368
Non-current liabilities	
Long term loan (20,000 + 8,850)	28,850
Current liabilities	
Trade and other payables (9,183 + 4,831)	14,014
Tax (1,059 + 311)	1,370
	15,384
Total liabilities	44,234
Total equity and liabilities	139,602

Workings

(W1) Goodwill

	£000
Consideration	26,680
Non-controlling interest at acquisition (40% × 37,800)	15,120
Net assets of Jones Ltd at acquisition	
6,000 + 4,000 + 19,800 + (43,470 − 35,470)	(37,800)
Goodwill	4,000
Impairment (10% × 4,000)	(400)
Goodwill in SFP	3,600

(W2) NCI

	£000
Share capital acquired (40% × 6,000)	2,400
Share premium acquired (40% × 4,000)	1,600
Retained earnings (40% × 25,200)	10,080
Fair value adjustment (40% × 8,000)	3,200
NCI	17,280

(W3) Retained earnings

	£000
Alasmith plc	40,248
Jones Ltd – post-acquisition profits attributable to Alasmith plc	
(25,200 − 19,800 = 5,400 × 60%)	3,240
Impairment	(400)
Group retained earnings	43,088

TASK 6 (8 MARKS)

Ratios

Quick ratio

$$\frac{\text{Current assets} - \text{inventory}}{\text{Current liabilities}} \qquad \frac{6{,}440 - 4{,}200}{2{,}800} \qquad 0.8{:}1$$

Inventories holding period

$$\frac{\text{Inventories}}{\text{Cost of sales}} \times 365 \qquad \frac{4{,}200}{8{,}716} \times 365 \qquad 175.9 \text{ days}$$

Trade receivables collection period

$$\frac{\text{Trade receivables}}{\text{Revenue}} \times 365 \qquad \frac{2{,}095}{14{,}994} \times 365 \qquad 51 \text{ days}$$

Interest cover

$$\frac{\text{Operating profit}}{\text{Finance costs}} \qquad \frac{2{,}700}{274} \qquad 9.9 \text{ times}$$

TASK 7 (22 MARKS)

(a) (i) **Identify whether the ratio is better or worse compared to the previous year.**

(5 marks)

(ii) **Explain what this may tell you about the company.** (15 marks)

The **gross profit ratio** has improved.

More gross profit is being generated from sales.

Improvement may be due to increasing the sales price per unit or decreasing the cost of sales or both. This could also be due to a change in the product mix or a new supplier contract.

The **expenses/revenue ratio** has improved.

The company has managed to improve its sales/expense mix, which will improve operating profits.

This could be due to a cost reduction programme, such as restricting pay rises, making staff redundant, changing stationery suppliers or reducing the costs of credit control (as examples). However, it could simply be that the business is able to sell more goods without incurring extra cost as it was operating with spare capacity in the prior year.

The **return on equity** has improved.

More net profit is being generated from the equity invested in the company.

This is due to an increase in reported profits in the current year without any increases in share capital.

The **gearing ratio** has deteriorated.

This could cause problems obtaining loans in the future as highly geared companies are more risky investment propositions for lenders.

Given the rise in return on equity it appears likely that growth has been funded using additional long term loan finance. As long as the company generates sufficient profit to cover interest repayments then this should not cause any problems for investors.

The **current ratio** has improved.

This means the business has more liquid assets in comparison to liabilities, meaning Manity Ltd is better able to pay its short term liabilities.

This has likely been caused by the improvements in profits, which should be generating more cash for the business. It could also be that some current liabilities were settled with new loan finance raised.

(b)   A recommendation, advising Coleen whether or not to invest:

Coleen should be advised **to invest**. **Gearing has deteriorated** but **overall profitability has improved** and the company appears to have made **good use of the capital invested**.

(2 marks)